THE LOONIEST GAMES! THE MEANEST TEAMS! THE SNEAKIEST PLAYERS!

THE FOOTBALL HALL OF SHAME

Q. How did a convicted burglar help steal a game for the New England Patriots? (see chapter on ... EVERY TRICK IN THE BOOK)

Q. In what Bowl game did the winners lose their shirts—and their pants, shoes, and helmets? (see chapter on ... TOILET BOWLS)

Q. How did Richard Nixon help the Washington Redskins lose their 1971 playoff game? (see chapter on ... SIDELINE SIDEWINDERS)

Q. Why did Stanford walk off the field with eight minutes left in the very first Rose Bowl game? (see chapter on ... FIRST DOWNERS)

Q. How did Larry "The Wild Man" Eisenhauer make a terrifying theatrical debut on a Boston kiddie show? (see chapter on ... TACKLING DUMMIES)

Books by Bruce Nash and Allan Zullo

The Baseball Hall of Shame™
The Baseball Hall of Shame™ 2
The Baseball Hall of Shame™ 3
The Baseball Hall of Shame™ 4
The Football Hall of Shame™
The Golf Hall of Shame™
The Sports Hall of Shame™
Baseball Confidential™
The Misfortune 500™

Published by POCKET BOOKS

THE
FOOTBALL
HALL OF SHAME

by

BRUCE NASH AND ALLAN ZULLO

BERNIE WARD, CURATOR

POCKET BOOKS

New York   London   Toronto   Sydney   Tokyo   Singapore

This book is dedicated to all college and pro players, head coaches, team personnel, officials, and fans who are big enough to laugh at their own foibles and screw-ups.

An *Original* publication of POCKET BOOKS

POCKET BOOKS, a division of Simon & Schuster Inc.
1230 Avenue of the Americas, New York, NY 10020

ISBN: 0-671-69135-X

First Pocket Books trade paperback printing September 1986

10 9 8 7 6

POCKET and colophon are registered trademarks
of Simon & Schuster, Inc.

THE FOOTBALL HALL OF SHAME is a registered trademark
of Nash and Zullo Productions, Inc.

Printed in the U.S.A.

ACKNOWLEDGMENT

We wish to thank all the fans, players, coaches, and sportswriters who contributed nominations.

We are especially grateful to those players and coaches, past and present, who shared a few laughs with us as they recounted the inglorious moments that earned them a place in The Football Hall of SHAME.

This book couldn't have been completed without the outstanding research of Al Kermisch, or the kindness of Ernest Clevenger, president of Faulkner University in Montgomery, Alabama, and Dick Cohen, president of the Sports Bookshelf in Ridgefield, Connecticut, both of whom allowed us access to their wonderful collections of football books.

We also appreciate the special efforts of Joe Horrigan and Ann Mangus of The Pro Football Hall of Fame in Canton, Ohio; Bob Carroll, president of the Professional Football Researchers Association; Bob Kirlin, president of the College Football Researchers Association; Tim Williams, of the NFL Alumni Association; and Eleanor Arnold.

In addition, we want to thank all the sportswriters, sports information directors, librarians, archivists, and fans who provided us with needed information and material. Special thanks go to: Brad Angers, Jim Campbell, George Castle, Loren Chamberlain, Larry Dale, Glenn Fess, Jim Ford, Frank Garofalo, Joe Gordon, Ellie Harness, Jamie Kimbrough, Larry Landman, Glen Miller, Dave Pellitier, Helen Ryan, Marc Ryan, Bill Whitmore, and Robert M. Willingham, Jr.

And for running interference for us and blocking many of the day-to-day hassles so we could finish this book, we give our love to Sophie Nash and Kathy Zullo.

CONTENTS

KICKING OFF

After paying a lighthearted tribute to the national pastime with our books *The Baseball Hall of SHAME* and *The Baseball Hall of SHAME 2*, it's time for us to give America's favorite spectator sport the discredit it deserves.

For nearly a century, football's swivel-hipped runners, golden-armed passers, clean-cut All-Americas, and undefeated conference champions have been immortalized. But let's face it, winners and heroes are *boring!* The things that really make the game so rousing, exciting, and entertaining are the muffed handoffs, the dropped passes, the shanked punts, the missed blocks.

Until now, the buffoons, the cheats, the flakes, and the boneheads have escaped the spotlight. They hid their shame in the huddle and concealed their embarrassment under their helmets. But no longer. We have their numbers—and a niche for each of them in The Football Hall of SHAME.

Football fans demanded such a shrine and even blitzed us with scores of nominations. Our own ongoing research into sports shame has uncovered many more little-known ignoble incidents and hilarious happenings in college football and in the National Football League, the American Football League, the United States Football League, and the World Football League.

After sifting through all the nominations, we selected those that had the best chance for enshrinement. Then we checked the accuracy of these accounts by scouring record books, archival material, and newspaper microfilm at The Football Hall of Fame Library in Canton, Ohio and the Library of Congress in Washington, D.C. To further help us verify the facts concerning nominees, we mobilized members of the Professional Football Researchers Association (of which we are members) and the sports information directors and librarians at various colleges and universities. When possible, we conducted personal interviews with the nominees themselves. Those nominations that met our unique standards were then chosen for induction.

All of the new inductees we spoke with shared a few chuckles with us as they relived their moments of infamy. It didn't matter if they were big names or not.

George Connor, the former Chicago Bears star linebacker, who made a most dubious debut in pro football, laughed when he was informed of his induction. "So I've gone from the Hall of Fame to the Hall of Shame," he said. "Wait until the guys hear about this."

Hall of Fame quarterback Y.A. Tittle, who lost more than his dignity in his most embarrassing play in college, said he felt honored to be inducted. But he added, "I don't know whether or not I'm glad you reminded me of that particular moment."

Many former players who had long been forgotten were delighted to hear they had been selected for induction. At least, they reasoned, they would be remembered for something—even if it was a shameful but funny moment.

Said former Boston Patriots defensive end Larry "The Wild Man" Eisenhauer, who made football's tackiest tackle, "I'm really in the Hall of Shame? Gee, I can't wait to tell my friends about this."

Some of the incidents we researched turned out to be apocryphal and, thus, were automatically rejected. Other incidents were ones that the nominees wished had never happened. Said Dan Devine, former coach at Missouri and Notre Dame, who delivered one of the most mortifying pep talks ever, "Some football stories seem to get exaggerated in the telling over the years until there's hardly any truth left. Unfortunately, my most embarrassing moment really did happen."

Just what does it mean to be in The Football Hall of SHAME? It's a special recognition of a moment we can all identify with—and laugh about—because each of us has fouled up at one time or another. We don't play favorites. We dishonor both the superstars and the bozos. As our motto says: "Fame *and* shame are part of the game."

FIRST DOWNERS

Rookies dream about what their glorious first game will bring. They see themselves blasting through the line for the winning touchdown in the final seconds, or leaping high in the air for the game-saving interception. That's the fantasy. The reality is that in their debuts, they often disgrace themselves so badly that they carry the stigma with them the rest of their careers—which can be a whole lot shorter than they planned. For "The Most Inauspicious Debuts," The Football Hall of SHAME inducts the following:

LEON HART

End • Notre Dame Fighting Irish • Sept. 28, 1946

In Leon Hart's first game in a Notre Dame uniform, he displayed the raw power that later made him a consensus All-America and a Heisman Trophy winner.

He drove forward with his head down and flattened the man in front of him. Unfortunately, the man he flattened was teammate Bob Livingstone, who was knocked unconscious by the hit-and-run encounter.

Summoned by coach Frank Leahy midway through a game against Illinois, the wide-eyed Hart eagerly listened to his mentor. "Leon, you're only a 17-year-old freshman," Leahy said. "This is your first game and I expect you to be nervous. You're up against older, more experienced opponents. But remember, if I didn't have confidence in you, I wouldn't send you into the game. Now, get in there at right end for Zilly."

The supercharged youth headed full throttle for the huddle and crashed smack dab into Livingstone, a halfback who was returning to the bench for a rest. Livingstone went down in a heap.

When he was revived a few minutes later, he shook his aching head

and said, "I've never been hit that hard before. That kid's going to be all right."

"Yeh," agreed Notre Dame trainer Hughie Burns, applying a bandage to Livingstone's chin, "but first we gotta teach him whose side he's on."

TERRY BRADSHAW

Quarterback • Pittsburgh Steelers • Sept. 20, 1970

When Terry Bradshaw went to Pittsburgh as the first college player selected in the 1970 NFL draft, the Steelers hailed him as their savior. Fans sang the praises of the $300,000 rookie who had passed for more than 7,000 yards at Louisiana Tech.

The Steel City had reason to celebrate. Its team had not won a championship in the previous 35 years, and had finished 1–13 in 1969. In Bradshaw, fans and players alike saw a redeemer who could lead the perennial losers on a march to the promised land—the Super Bowl.

A near-capacity crowd showed up at Three Rivers Stadium to watch the NFL debut of the new miracle worker. But Bradshaw played so terribly the fans went home wondering if he was anything more than a false idol.

Bradshaw must have sensed impending disaster. Before stepping onto the field to face the Houston Oilers, he threw up. Some spectators probably felt like doing the same thing when they saw the way he passed.

Some of his tosses were wobbly. Others were on the money but were thrown too hard for the receivers to catch. On one play, receiver Ron Shanklin broke free for what should have been a touchdown pass, only to have the ball slip off Bradshaw's sweaty hand and drift in a high lazy arc. Shanklin had to wait forever for the ball to come down. When he finally caught it, he was smeared 20 yards short of the goal line.

Bradshaw misfired on 9 straight passes and tossed an interception that led the Oilers to their second touchdown. Adding to his embarrassment, Bradshaw also caused a safety for the Oilers by stepping out of the end zone while setting up to pass.

Late in the third quarter, with Houston leading 16–0, Steeler coach Chuck Noll called Bradshaw to his side and told him he was being benched. Substitute Terry Hanratty went into the game and Bradshaw, who had completed only 4 of 16 passes for a total of 70 yards, slumped on a folding wooden chair.

After the game (won by the Oilers 19–7), Bradshaw told reporters, "The benching put a big lump in my throat. I told myself, 'What now, big shot? Everybody was counting on you and you blew it. You better hide when you get to that locker room.'

"I couldn't hit the side of a barn. I was yelling at the guys in the huddle, but it was false chatter. I kept saying, 'Let's go! Let's go!' But deep down I knew that we weren't going anyplace."

Bradshaw eventually atoned for his early football sins. From 1975 to 1980, he lead the Steelers to 4 Super Bowl victories, capping a sparkling career. But he will never forget his NFL baptism when he played like a lost soul.

GEORGE CONNOR

Tackle-Linebacker • Chicago Bears • 1948–55

George Connor was a little slow to understand why his initiation into pro football was so painful. Opposing linemen kept belting him in the jaw. Eventually, though, those haymakers knocked some sense into the rookie.

In his first few pro games, Connor was the backup tackle for Fred Davis. Whenever Davis needed a rest, he would raise his hand in the huddle. That was the signal for Connor to substitute for him after the next play.

Connor's initial taste of life in the trenches came during an exhibition game. When he saw Davis' arm go up, Connor grabbed his helmet, watched the end of the play, and raced out onto the field. On his first play from scrimmage, Connor sprang into action—and was promptly punched in the mouth by the opposing lineman. Connor was smarting from the blow, but he thought that maybe this was the typical welcome given to rookies.

Later in the same game, Connor again replaced Davis and set up against a different lineman. But the results were the same; once again, he was socked in the face.

"It was the same story during those first few games," Connor, now a Hall of Famer, recalled. "Every time I went in the game, the guy opposite me smashed me in the mouth. I thought maybe they didn't like me personally or maybe they didn't like rookies from Notre Dame. I was afraid that if this was the way pro football was played, I wasn't sure I wanted to keep playing."

Finally, early in the fifth game, Connor wised up. This time, when Davis raised his hand in the huddle, Connor kept his eyes on Davis rather than the play itself. When the ball was snapped, the rookie saw Davis lunge across the line, punch the opposing lineman in the face, and trot off toward the Bear bench. It was then that Connor realized he was paying for all of Davis' dirty work.

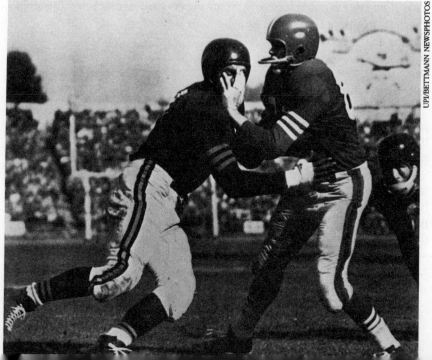

"The linemen didn't pay any attention to who was opposite them," recalled Connor. "They were just mad that somebody had punched them. So from that moment on, whenever I substituted for Davis, I'd tell the opposing lineman, 'Fred Davis out, George Connor in.' I never got hit again.

"After that game, I asked Fred why he was doing that to me and he just laughed in my face and said, 'Why did it take you 5 games to catch on?' "

MUNCIE FLYERS

Oct. 3, 1920

After their performance in the inaugural week of pro football's first major league, the Muncie Flyers should have been arrested for fraud.

The Flyers weren't pros; they were cons. The team duped the paying fans into believing it was a strong, tough and skilled football team—but only until the spectators saw the squad play.

The Flyers traveled to Rock Island, Illinois to meet the Independents in the debut of the American Professional Football Association (forerunner to the NFL). But in the opening minutes of the game, it became crystal clear that the Flyers deserved to be grounded for masquerading as professionals.

They were so inept at blocking and executing plays that they wouldn't have been able to lay a finger on a touch football team. Muncie turned the first quarter into a travesty.

After the opening kickoff, the inept Flyers couldn't move the ball anywhere but backward and were forced to punt. Rock Island tackle Ed Shaw blocked the kick, and teammate Arnie Wyman scooped up the ball and ran 35 yards for the league's very first touchdown.

A few minutes later, Muncie again sputtered badly on offense and punter Ken Huffine, from behind his own goal line, tried to kick out of trouble. This time, Rock Island's other tackle, Walt Buland, blocked the punt and then fell on it in the end zone for the second touchdown.

Following the kickoff, the futile Flyers stalled again deep in their own territory, so Huffine attempted another punt. For the third time, it was blocked, and the Independents hit pay dirt to make the score 21–0 in the first quarter. It would have been better if the Flyers had just handed the ball over to Rock Island after fourth down.

The Independents let everyone play—they could have suited up the water boy—and coasted to an easy 45–0 romp. Muncie performed so poorly that its next scheduled opponent, the Decatur Staleys (who later became the Chicago Bears), immediately cancelled the game. Decatur didn't want to waste its time beating up on wimps.

The Flyers' financial backers needed no more proof that the team was a loser and pulled out. The team quickly folded. Some histories of the NFL fail to even mention the Muncie Flyers. Is it any wonder?

REX KEELING

Punter ▪ Cincinnati Bengals ▪ Dec. 1, 1968

Rex Keeling's debut as a punter for the Cincinnati Bengals was so pitiful that coach Paul Brown actually cut him at halftime.

Keeling was in Alabama selling cars for his father when he got a call from Brown. The coach explained that the Bengals' regular punter, Dale Livingston, had just been called up for military duty and that the team needed a punter for the final three games of the season. Keeling, who had tried out for the Bengals as a free agent the previous summer, jumped at the chance to play pro football

He should have stayed in the car business.

Although he hadn't punted in months, Keeling was booting punts of 50 yards during practice the week before his first game. But in his pro debut, playing against the Boston Patriots, he kicked for barely half that distance. Keeling averaged only 28.3 yards on six punts and had one partially blocked.

His most ignominious moment came late in the second quarter when, on a fake punt at midfield, he bobbled the snap, tried to run with the ball, and finally threw it forward underhanded. It fell to the ground. The play was ruled a fumble, and Boston took possession on the Cincinnati 45-yard line. Keeling's bungle set up a touchdown for the Patriots, who built a 26–0 lead after two quarters.

In the locker room at halftime, Brown was livid. The raging coach blasted Keeling for letting the pressure of the pros get to him. "This game is just too big for you, Rex," he scolded him in front of the team. "You just can't handle it. You're gone!" With that, Brown turned to his son Mike, a team executive, and said, "Write this boy out a check for what we owe him." Then, in a voice loud enough for all to hear, Brown muttered, "That's what I get for trying to make a kicker out of a used-car salesman."

In recalling his brief pro career, Keeling said he had a feeling Brown was fed up with him when the coach called for the fake punt. "I couldn't find anybody open so I took off, and this 300-pound monster caught me and knocked me into a TV camera and almost killed me," said Keeling. "I've always believed Brown called that play just to get even with me."

ROSE BOWL

Jan. 1, 1902

The Rose Bowl's very first game was such a mismatch that the slaughtered team gave up and quit with eight minutes left to play. Red-faced Bowl officials couldn't handle their embarrassment and didn't stage another bowl game for fourteen years.

The oldest post-season bowl debuted in 1902 as part of Pasadena's annual Rose Festival. The Stanford Cardinals were selected to represent the West against the eastern powerhouse, the Michigan Wolverines. The awesome Wolverines had won all 11 of their games by racking up an incredible 555 points while shutting out every opponent. Their defense was so impenetrable that the longest gain against Michigan all year was only 15 yards.

Clearly, the weaker, smaller Stanford team did not belong on the same field with the snarling Wolverines, whose vicious tackling, blocking, and running injured enough Cardinals to fill a hospital ward. "We couldn't stand the terrific smashing of those bulldog fighters," said Stanford trainer "Dad" Moulton. "After they had laid out our best men, they had everything their own way."

As Michigan bludgeoned its way to a 49–0 lead, the Stanford players didn't need their college education to know when to chuck it in. Enough was enough. Actually, 49–0 was more than enough.

So with eight minutes remaining, Stanford captain R.S. Fisher staggered over to Michigan captain Hugh White and said, "If you are willing, we are ready to quit." White, a brutal left tackle showing a touch of compassion for the first time all day, said that was fine and dandy with him.

The mortified Tournament of Roses Association decided that football should be dropped from the annual program until California could produce a team that wouldn't shame the West.

So what replaced football during the annual Rose Festival? Believe it or not, they ran chariot races! Amateur drivers nearly killed each other so professional drivers took over—until the cry of "fix" tainted the races.

The Tournament of Roses Association finally decided that football wasn't so bad after all. In 1916, after memories of its deplorable debut had finally faded, football returned to the Rose Bowl.

THE BOTTOM OF
THE BARREL

It's a good thing that losing, cellar-dwelling teams don't have commemorative stamps made of them. People wouldn't know which side to spit on. These teams don't belong on a gridiron; they belong in a Keystone Cops movie. For "The Worst Teams of All Time," The Football Hall of SHAME inducts the following:

DALLAS TEXANS

1952

The Dallas Texans were an NFL joke—a very bad joke.

With a roster of wide-eyed greenhorns and broken-down old hands, the Texans were saddled with a legacy of failure. When their first and only season was half over, they were kicked out of town and forced to wander the league as vagabonds. At year's end they disbanded, becoming the last NFL team to fold.

The Texans were the offspring of losers, the New York Yanks, who lost so many games and dollars for owner Ted Collins that he gave the franchise back to the NFL. A few weeks later, commissioner Bert Bell awarded the franchise to millionaire Giles Miller in Texas, which had long been a hotbed for college and high school football. Declared Miller, "There is room enough in Texas for all kinds of football." But not bad football.

On opening day, only 17,499 curious spectators watched the New York Giants welcome the Texans to the league with a 24–6 drubbing. The fans had seen more than enough, and the Cotton Bowl turned into an empty echo chamber during the next 3 home games. Unable to meet his financial obligations, Miller turned control of the team over to the league. The squad was moved to Hershey, Pennsylvania, where it held loosely organized practices. For the second half of the year, the Texans traveled the country as an itinerant road team, although they performed more like a vaudeville road show.

They drew more flies than fans. While losing 11 of 12 games, they scored a per-game average of only 15 points and gave up a whopping 35 points per game. They finished last in total yards, missed 7 of 27 extra point attempts, and failed on all four field goal attempts.

Coach Jim Phelan had no luck with the kicking game. He tried turning collegiate passing star Don Klosterman into a kicking specialist even though the rookie wanted to be the team's quarterback. Unfortunately, Klosterman missed a field goal and was cut the next day. Before leaving, Klosterman claimed he deserved another chance. Later, when the team reviewed the game film, Phelan stopped the projector after seeing Klosterman's failed kick. The coach backed up the reel and ran the play over again. "There," he told his players. "Who says I didn't give Klosterman a second chance?"

One reason why the team stunk was that Phelan hated practice as much as the players did. Once, after they ran a few plays without fouling up, Phelan stopped practice, loaded everybody on a bus, and took them to the racetrack. Some players didn't take games all that seriously either. Rookie guard George Robison, for one, was always cracking jokes in the huddle. He certainly had plenty of material just from watching the team play. One of his favorite lines was asking a teammate in the huddle, "What comes after 75?" The teammate would answer, "76," and Robison would come back with, "That's the spirit!"

The Texans' only win ever came at the expense of the Chicago Bears in, of all places, Akron, Ohio. The game was slated as the second part of a Thanksgiving doubleheader. The morning game pitted two high school teams, who played to a full house. Then almost everyone went home before the start of the pro contest.

Looking over the few fans in the stands, Phelan told his troops, "Instead of running under the goal posts for introductions, let's just go up and shake hands with everybody. It would be faster. It won't take more than a minute or two."

Chicago coach George Halas took the Texans for patsies and played his second stringers until the Bears trailed 20–2. The Texans held on for a shocking 27–23 victory. Flushed with success, the Texans prepared for their next opponent, the Philadelphia Eagles. Not wanting to be a victim of an upset, Eagle coach Greasy Neale sent a scout to watch the Texans practice in Hershey. When the scout returned, he told Neale, "You're not going to believe this, but they were playing volleyball over the goal posts." The Texans reverted to form and lost 38–21 to the Eagles. In their very last game, the Texans were trounced 41–6 by the Detroit Lions. Late in the game with the score 41–0, they finally made a touchdown, prompting Phelan to shout, "We've got them on the run now!"

When the season ended, half the Texans—twenty players—quit pro football. Among them were nine rookies who wished they had stayed in college. Twelve others went to the league's newest franchise, the Baltimore Colts. Lamented Phelan, "We got all the breaks—and they were all bad."

MACALESTER COLLEGE SCOTS

1974–80

The Macalester Scots twisted Vince Lombardi's philosophy inside out. To them losing wasn't everything; it was the only thing.

Like an unoiled machine misfiring on all cylinders, Macalester sputtered to 50 consecutive losses and set a National Collegiate Athletic Association record in futility. The school did one better than its famous alumnus, Walter Mondale. He lost only 49 states in the 1984 Presidential election.

Like Mondale, the Scots didn't just lose. They lost big. In 1977, they dropped all 8 games by a combined point total of 532–39. That year, they roared to a quick 6–0 advantage over Concordia-Moorhead but couldn't hold the lead and fell 97–6. In 1978, they were blown away by such scores as 61–0, 62–7, 46–0, 51–7, and 55–13.

Macalester, a St. Paul, Minnesota liberal arts school of 1,700 students noted for academic excellence, fielded a football team of martyrs, who were battered and bruised in body and psyche. The official school colors of black and orange should have been changed to black and blue. Most of the players were freshmen and sophomores because the juniors and seniors were either too hurt, too discouraged, or too smart to continue playing.

Others, perhaps nursing masochistic tendencies, stuck it out as the losses piled up like autumn leaves. Some players had played four full seasons for the team without ever taking a lead into the locker room at halftime. And with each embarrassing setback, the pressure grew, as did media attention.

"It was so bad," recalled coach Tom Hosier, "that in a scrimmage against a junior college, we went in the huddle on offense and I thought we'd never come out of it. We were that afraid to lose."

Their most successful offensive play was downing the kickoff in the end zone; it gained 20 yards every time. Occasionally, they tried to pull a surprise play, like running up the middle on first down. Sometimes the Scots caught their opponents off guard and racked up a yard or two.

One nihilistic student fan said, "We had to give up on our punt-return strategy—down the left side or down the right—because a lot of the guys couldn't grasp the concept involved."

There was talk at the school of dropping football—something the team's running backs had been doing with regularity for several years. But then came Macalester's biggest game ever. The nation watched and held its breath as the Scots attempted to break the old NCAA record of 39 consecutive losses when they faced St. John's of Collegeville, Minnesota, on October 28, 1978.

Despite the movement on campus to scrap the football program in favor of soccer—or anything else—about 3,000 enthusiastic, placard-bearing fans showed up at Macalester Stadium for the historic event. Banners proclaimed, "We're No. 1" and "Go Big Mac" and warned Notre Dame to watch out. When the Scots recovered a fumble and then completed a third-down pass in the first quarter, the fans began shouting, "Orange Bowl! Orange Bowl! Orange Bowl!"

But the student body radicals had their own chant: "Ho, Ho, Ho Chi Minh, Macalester will never win!"

It sure looked like they were right. On the first play from scrimmage, St. John's Mark McCullen ran 72 yards for a touchdown. A Macalester defender had a shot at stopping McCullen near the 10-yard line, but was neatly and unwittingly blocked by an official who did not see him coming. The longest run of the day for Macalester—and the one that brought the biggest cheer—occurred when the campus dog, a 2-year-old mongrel, scampered onto the field.

The Scots were clobbered, 44–0. The record was theirs—possibly forever. Despite the rout, it was clear that the Macalester defense had grown stronger. The year before, St. John's had beaten the Scots 70–0.

With every loss following the St. John's whipping, Macalester set a new inglorious collegiate mark. But we all wake up from nightmares. For Macalester, the nightmare ended on September 6, 1980 against Mount Scenario College of Ladysmith, Wisconsin.

With 11 seconds left in a 14–14 game, Scots freshman kicker Bob Kaye was called upon to boot a 23-yard field goal that would win the game. His kick wobbled like a drunk on a window ledge and skimmed through the goal post just inside the left upright. But neatness doesn't count. The kick was good. The Macalester Scots had won a football game. The 50-game losing streak was over. "There were parties all over campus," recalled athletic director Dennis Keihn. "We had champagne on ice for the occasion. Trouble is, it had been on ice for six years."

When coach Tom Hosier was asked what the team would do for an encore, he declared, "Win again next week!" After one victory, overconfidence had already set in. It would have been nice to report that the Scots went on to win two in a row. But they lost their next game 20–7, halting their one-game winning streak. It had to end sometime . . . but so soon?

NORTHWESTERN WILDCATS

1976–82

It's ironic that Evanston, Illinois is the home of the Women's Christian Temperance Union and Northwestern University. For this is the town with a collegiate football tradition awful enough to drive you to drink.

From 1976 until midway into the 1982 season, Northwestern won only 3 games, tied one, and lost 65. It holds the major college record of 34 consecutive defeats and has achieved only three winning seasons in the last twenty-five years.

The losing tradition is long-established. In fact, no major institution of higher education has worn an athletic hair shirt for so many autumns. The gates of football purgatory open directly into Dyche Stadium, home of the Wildcats, or (as they are more affectionately known) the Mildcats.

"It's an unhappy and doleful feeling knowing the only way you're going to win is if everyone on the other team dies of cholera," lamented one long-suffering fan.

Because of the Wildcats' poor play, there was talk of changing the name of their conference from the Big Ten to the Big Nine-and-a-half.

Until recently, most of the blame rested with an administration that thought losing enhanced the academic reputation of the school. As the smallest, most expensive, and academically toughest university in the conference, Northwestern, unlike other schools, poured money into education rather than its football program.

Northwestern recruited students who were more concerned about grade point averages than wire service polls; who worked harder for A's than first downs. So what if the team ranked last in the standings? The school ranks second to Harvard in the number of alumni who are officers in Fortune 500 companies. Perhaps that's why the students' favorite cheer during a typical loss is: "That's all right/ That's okay/ They're gonna work for *us* some day!"

Humanitarians wanted to stop the weekly slaughter of the outmatched

Wildcats and suggested the school drop out of the Big Ten. The other conference members wouldn't even entertain the thought. Playing Northwestern has been like getting a week off, a guaranteed "W" in the record book, and a chance to fatten the stats. The schools have loved Northwestern—especially from 1976 through 1981 when its record read like an obscenity in computer BASIC: 1–10, 1–10, 1–10, 0–11, 0–11.

Northwestern suffered its most humiliating year in 1981 when it was outscored 505–82—an average shellacking of 46–7. During a 6-game stretch, the Wildcats were shut out five times, causing the *Chicago Tribune* to observe: "On the list of vital occupations, a Northwestern placekicker is tied for last place with the guy who runs an Edsel muffler shop."

Cheerleader Steve DePalma confessed to the press, "We gave up a long time ago on trying to get the crowds cheering for touchdowns and field goals. Instead, we now try to get them excited when the Wildcats actually catch a punt."

It was the year when fans didn't encourage the Northwestern defense to "Stop 'em!" Instead they shouted, "Slow 'em down!" It was the year fans told freshman quarterback Kevin Villars, "You're no good" and he replied, "You're right." It was the year when some Northwestern sage shimmied up the highway sign "Interstate 94" and added, "Northwestern 0." Above all, it was the year when the Wildcats broke the old major collegiate record of 28 consecutive defeats.

On November 7, 1981, Northwestern hosted the Michigan State Spartans, who owned a mediocre 3–5 record but were nonetheless 28-point favorites. To etch their name in the record books, the Wildcats were in a must-lose situation. And lose they did.

After the coin flip was won by the Spartans, after the opening kickoff was returned to the Wildcats' 24-yard line, after Northwestern's best defensive player was knocked out of the game on the first play from scrimmage, and after the Spartans scored a touchdown on fourth down with barely 2 minutes gone in the game, things *really* got bad for Northwestern. Michigan State scored on all 7 of its possessions in the first half and led 41–0.

The fans didn't seem to care. They were having their own brand of fun. "You have to get drunk during the games because you can't watch otherwise," said a beer-swilling coed. Some students were throwing hot dogs into the band's tubas. Other fans were engaging in the school's traditional lark, girl passing. Male fans selected a coed and then passed her up over their heads to the top of the stands. The crowd chanted, "All the way! All the way!" as she was passed up. It was a mixed honor to be selected. Once the girl reached the last row, they shouted, "Over the top! Over the top!"

In the second half, a group of fans paraded with a banner carrying the message: "Hey, Mom. Keep the money, send a team."

When the Wildcats finally scored a touchdown in the third period, they broke a streak of 14 scoreless quarters. No one was happier than Willy the Wildcat, a student dressed in a football uniform and a feline head. At each game that year, he was locked in a cage, not to be released for a prance in the end zone, until the team scored. Fortunately, he was freed after each game during the scoreless skein or the cage door would have rusted shut and poor Willy would have starved to death.

Northwestern ended up losing 61–14 to break the futility record. Reported the *Detroit Free Press:* "The streak is at 29 and counting. It belongs to Northwestern, the team for which life always seems to be fourth and 21."

After the game, the fans attacked the goal posts. But the mob had as much trouble tearing down the uprights as the team did getting near them. "Typical Northwestern," mused a student. "It took us 50 minutes to do what any other school could do in a minute." Once the goal posts were torn down, they were carried through the sleepy streets of Evanston accompanied by the chant, "We are the worst! We are the worst!" Then the crowd threw the goal posts into Lake Michigan.

To the chagrin of the coaching staff, thirty-five prep prospects had been invited to the game. It was a rather inauspicious day to woo new players. No wonder the Wildcats had trouble recruiting talent. Who wanted to go to a school that was handed its head every week?

It looked like another sorry year in 1982 after Northwestern lost its first three games by a combined score of 106–26 and had accumulated minus 44 yards rushing. But after years of getting kicked around, they finally played a puppy-dog team, the Northern Illinois Huskies. Lo and behold, the Wildcats mauled the Huskies 31–6. The horrendous losing streak had ended after 34 straight defeats.

The victors gave the game ball to their coach, Dennis Green. They should have given it to the Northern Illinois bus driver for delivering the Huskies to the game.

TAMPA BAY BUCCANEERS

1976–77

No professional football team started out as miserably as the Tampa Bay Bucs. They lost their first 26 regular season games, 11 by shutout.

The Bucs were headed in the wrong direction even before the kickoff of their NFL debut. After completing their pre-game warmups in the Houston Astrodome, the team followed their coach, John McKay, off the field and into the concrete innards of the stadium. And there they promptly got lost.

Forty-five players, eight coaches, and assorted equipment men, trainers, and doctors wandered around befuddled, searching futilely for the locker room. Finally, a security guard found them and guided them back to their locker room. But by then, the Bucs had just a few minutes to get ready and return to the field for the start of the game.

As it turns out, the offense never did find the end zone and mustered only a paltry total of 108 yards in a 20–0 loss to the Houston Oilers.

The next week, the offense produced only 13 yards through the air. "The running backs ran like they were mud fences," complained McKay. Thirty-nine times in the game, Tampa Bay either failed to move the football or was thrown for a loss.

Not until the fourth game did the Bucs score their first touchdown— and it was pulled off by the defense on a 44-yard fumble recovery. Most of the Bucs' offensive punch was supplied by cornerback Mike Washington, who threw a fist and was ejected from the game. Afterward, McKay said, "We will be back, maybe not in this century, but we will be back."

Following their eighth straight loss, 28–19 to Kansas City, McKay lost his patience and temper. He thundered, "They were absolutely horrible and that's the nicest thing I can say about them."

The next week, Tampa Bay raised the hopes of its fans when the team tied Denver 10–10 in the third quarter. But the joy was short-lived. The Bucs lost, 48–13. McKay's frustration reached a peak; he refused to shake Denver coach John Ralston's hand after the game. Instead, McKay accused Ralston of running up the score, and hurled a bunch of obscenities at the Bronco coach. Meanwhile, Tampa's starting tight end Bob Moore summed up the feeling of the losing team, "Sometimes I feel as though I were on the aft deck of the Lusitania."

The following week, the New York Jets sacked Buc quarterbacks four times and took advantage of six turnovers to record their first shutout in thirteen years, 34–0.

In their final game of the year, a 31–14 clobbering by the New England Patriots, the Bucs became the only expansion team in NFL history to lose all the games in their first season. "I'll probably take a little time off," said a weary McKay, "and go hide someplace."

The Bucs started the second year off just like the first, scoring only one touchdown in the first 4 games. They lost for the second straight year to their expansion brothers, the Seattle Seahawks, this time 30–23, on 4 interceptions and 2 fumbles. In a game in which the Bucs' offense scored its most points ever, the defense decided to take the day off.

The next week, the Bucs lost to Green Bay, 13 to terrible. Said the *St. Petersburg Times:* "Continuing their unrelenting vendetta against victory, the Tampa Bay Bucs pulled out all the stops to ward off an impending win and kept their losing streak intact. The Bucs used timely penalties, fumbles, mental lapses and an absolutely pointless display of offensive football to further secure their position at the bottom of the NFL barrel."

They played rookies who were so inexperienced that some of them hadn't even lettered. Fans began hoping for 0-for-forever and wore T-shirts that read, "Go for 0." They cheered the visiting teams. They had little reason to cheer the Bucs. But on occasion they would applaud when the team did something spectacular—like making a particularly smooth entry onto the field.

Finally, 1,298 days after the Bucs were awarded an NFL franchise, they savored the taste of victory.

On December 11, 1977, the laughingstocks of the league won their very first game, a 33–14 romp over the hapless New Orleans Saints. Nothing could have been more horrendous for New Orleans. "What a nightmare!" declared Hank Stram, coach of the bedeviled Saints. "It's the worst experience of my coaching career. We're ashamed of our people, our fans, our organization."

SICK KICKS

Kickers think of themselves as game-winners who have the fate of their teams riding on their talented toes. But sometimes their fortunes are more like bad punts—shanked out of bounds. To the lousy kicker, hang time means how long it will take for irate fans to string him up, and the coffin corner is where they want to bury him. For "The Most Inept Kicking Performances," The Football Hall of SHAME inducts the following:

MIKE CLARK

Placekicker • Dallas Cowboys • Dec. 28, 1969

Mike Clark was responsible for the most embarrassing kickoff ever witnessed in an NFL play-off game.

Trailing the Cleveland Browns 38–7 after scoring a touchdown late in the contest, the Dallas Cowboys tried to get the ball back by having Clark attempt an onside kick.

The front line of the Browns tensed up in anticipation of the short kick while the Cowboys eagerly waited to pounce on the ball. Clark knew he had to hit the pigskin just right, squibbing it so that it would travel at least 10 yards but not much further. With total concentration, he trotted toward the ball, planted his left foot, and swung with his right.

The Cowboys charged forward and banged into the Browns. While some of the players blocked, others surged to where the ball should have been kicked. But it wasn't there. A frantic search began. No, it wasn't under a pile of Browns or a gang of Cowboys. The players finally spotted the ball, still standing upright where Clark had placed it—on the kicking tee. Clark had whiffed the kick!

His shoulders hunched, Clark just stood over the ball for a moment and shook his head as the Dallas boo-birds—already angry over the score—hooted and jeered.

The Cowboys were penalized 5 yards for being offside, so Clark attempted a second onside kick. This time he managed to kick the ball. Both teams dove for it as it bounced, but all the smashing helmets, hurling bodies, and clawing fingers were for naught. Clark's kick hadn't gone the required 10 yards. Once again, Dallas was penalized 5 yards.

By now, Clark could feel the heat steaming off the necks of his irritated teammates. He sure wasn't going to screw up on his third straight kickoff attempt. This time he had a foolproof plan. He ran up to the ball and booted it deep.

For this mortifying kicking episode, Clark was dishonored by the Dallas Bonehead Club. At the award ceremonies, Clark properly chastised himself by saying, "Everyone is entitled to make a mistake, but not in front of 70,000 spectators and a national TV audience."

RAFAEL SEPTIEN

Placekicker • Los Angeles Rams–Dallas Cowboys • 1977–Present

Rafael Septien has no peers—when it comes to making up lamebrained excuses for missed field goals.

His alibis are as weak as a squibbed kick off the crossbar and as weird as a paisley goal post.

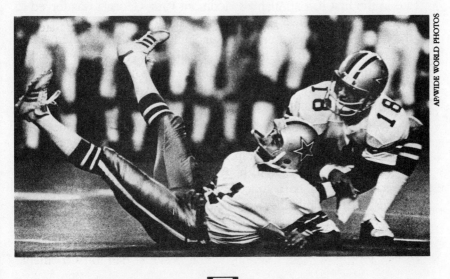

AP/WIDE WORLD PHOTOS

After he muffed 4 of 5 field goal attempts against the Houston Oilers on September 29, 1985, Septien didn't rely on the old, hackneyed excuses like "It was a bad snap" or "The holder messed up." Nope, Septien put the blame squarely on his shoulders. He confessed, "I was too busy reading my stats on the scoreboard."

Later, when he blew a field goal in a game at Texas Stadium, Septien had a ready explanation: "The grass was too tall." So was his tale of woe. Texas Stadium doesn't even have grass; its surface is artificial turf.

Once when he shanked a chip shot, he said it was because "the 30-second clock distracted me." Another time, he booted a wounded duck that fell far short of the uprights. His excuse? "My helmet was too tight and it was squeezing my brain. I couldn't think."

Septien has seldom blamed anyone else for his messed-up kicks. But once, when yet another field goal attempt went wide, he turned to his holder, quarterback Danny White, and said, "No wonder. You placed the ball upside down."

ARTHUR SULLIVAN

Punter · Georgia Bulldogs · Nov. 12, 1904

The Georgia Bulldogs and the Georgia Tech Yellow Jackets tangled in a play so shamefully crazy that both teams were literally climbing the wall. And it was all because of one of the most deplorable punts ever seen in a college game.

Late in the first half at Atlanta's Piedmont Park, Georgia was forced to punt from behind its own goal line. Since the goal posts back then were on the goal line, Georgia punter Arthur Sullivan was behind them when he kicked the ball. To his horror, the ball struck the crossbar with a sickening thud and bounded behind him over a 16-foot-high wooden wall. For several moments, the players stood still with blank expressions. They didn't know what to do. Because there were no end zones in those days, referee George Butler ruled the ball was still in play—and that triggered a mad scramble for the fence.

If a Georgia player could grab the ball, it would be only a 2-point safety against the Bulldogs. If, however, a Yellow Jacket were to gain possession, it would be a touchdown for Tech. The players on both teams rushed to climb the wall, made slippery by a recent rain. No sooner would a player make his way to the top than an opponent would grab his leg and pull him back down again.

Dozier Lowndes, a Georgia substitute, was not eligible to chase the ball because he wasn't in the lineup, but he did his part by fighting off two Tech players who tried to use a large stump near the wall for climbing. Finally, Sullivan of Georgia, Red Wilson of Tech, and referee Butler scaled the wall and began a frantic search for the ball in the clumps of bushes skirting a nearby lake. Meanwhile, the crowd waited anxiously for the outcome.

Wilson was the first to spot the ball, and pounced on it for a touchdown. Since Sullivan was looking elsewhere, the referee was the only witness to the score.

Not until Wilson reappeared at the top of the wall, clutching the pigskin, did the Tech fans erupt in cheers. The bizarre touchdown spurred the Yellow Jackets on to a 23–6 victory.

CLAIR SCOTT

Punter ▪ Indiana Hoosiers ▪ Nov. 8, 1913

Punters tend to get angry at themselves when one of their punts falls harmlessly into an opponent's end zone for a touchback. They should thank their lucky shoelaces they never suffered the fate of Clair Scott.

INDIANA UNIVERSITY ATHLETIC DEPARTMENT

He booted the worst punt in football history.

Scott's moment of infamy came during the Iowa Hawkeyes' 60–0 trouncing of his Indiana Hoosiers. Late in the second quarter, the Hoosiers were penned in on their own 3-yard line on fourth down. Standing back as far as he could in the Indiana end zone, Scott punted the pigskin with all his might.

The ball sailed high in the air—right into the teeth of a 50 mph gale. Iowa punt returner Leo Dick, who was waiting for the ball on the Indiana 25-yard line, noticed that the ball seemed to hang in the air over the 20-yard line. So he trotted in a few steps. But because of the stiff wind, the ball began to drift backward. So Dick trotted in a few more steps. But he was not much closer to the ball. It was now descending, and sailing steadily backward.

Dick broke into a wild dash and finally caught the ball—right in the Indiana end zone—for a touchdown!

SEAN LANDETA

Punter • New York Giants • Jan. 5, 1986

It's understandable if you swing at a baseball or even a golf ball and miss. But how does a punter miss a football? Ask Sean Landeta. He's responsible for the most disgraceful punt in NFL play-off history.

Midway through the first quarter of a scoreless showdown between the New York Giants and Chicago Bears in the Windy City, Landeta was sent in to punt from his own goal line.

As the Bears launched an all-out rush, Landeta took the snap and released the ball to kick it. Incredibly, he swung his leg and missed the ball! The pigskin barely grazed his instep, skipped off horizontally to his right, then dropped to the turf. Chicago defender Shaun Gayle scooped up the ball at the 5-yard line and scampered into the end zone for the first touchdown of the game. Landeta's blunder went down as a minus-7-yard punt, although it should have been listed as an attempted punt.

Landeta felt like climbing into a hole—the 7–0 hole he had created for his Giants, who went on to lose 21–0. "I couldn't believe it," he said. "It's something that never happened to me before. I mean, you don't even miss a ball just fooling around."

He claimed the wind gusted just as he was about to punt and made the ball do tricks on his drop. It's strange that in all the decades of pro football the wind waited until this pressure-packed game—watched by a rapt national TV audience—to cause the first player in memory to strike out on a punt.

Landeta had suffered another indignity three weeks earlier in a big game against the Dallas Cowboys for the NFC East title. Set to punt deep inside his 5-yard line, Landeta couldn't get his punt off because of a fierce Cowboy rush. So he tried his version of a forward pass. He underhanded the ball right into the back of a teammate, setting up the winning touchdown for Dallas.

BOOTH LUSTEG

Placekicker • Buffalo Bills • Oct. 16, 1966

No placekicker ever booted himself out of town more shamefully than Booth Lusteg.

When he played for the Buffalo Bills in 1966, Lusteg never won over the fans, even though he led the AFL in scoring that year with 98 points.

He endured a love-hate relationship with Buffalo that was less love and more hate. It was his own fault. For starters, Lusteg missed half of his 38 field goal attempts. But the one he blew against the San Diego Chargers really did him in.

All the Bills needed to wrap up the victory in the closing minute of a 17-all tie was an easy 23-yard field goal. What they got from Lusteg was a kick that sailed wide like an out-of-control Frisbee. The game ended in a tie.

Afterward, Lusteg was ambling along the sidewalk a few blocks away from the stadium when a passing car slammed on its brakes. Four boiling mad fans leaped out of the car and confronted the kicker. "Are you Booth Lusteg?" one of them demanded to know.

Even though he was outnumbered and could see the anger in their eyes, Lusteg unwisely said, "Yeah, that's me." For his honesty, one of the fans punched Lusteg right in the nose before they all jumped back into their car and sped away.

A witness reported the incident to the police the next day, but when the cops asked Lusteg about it, he declined comment.

"Did it really happen?" Jack Horrigan, the club's vice president, asked him.

"Of course," Lusteg replied.

"Then why didn't you tell the cops about it?"

"I didn't tell them," Lusteg said, "because I had it coming."

He had something else coming at the end of the year. His release.

EVERY TRICK IN THE BOOK

If good sportsmanship were a conference requirement, some teams would have to forfeit. That's because they make an end run around the rule book. It's part of their game plan—one developed by Machiavelli himself. They are so unfair they don't even know how to call for a fair catch. For "The Sneakiest Chicanery Ever Perpetrated," The Football Hall of SHAME inducts the following:

GEORGIA BULLDOGS

Oct. 26, 1912

The Georgia Bulldogs used a pair of coveralls to pull the denim over the eyes of the Alabama Crimson Tide.

When the Bulldogs lined up on their own 20-yard line for the first play from scrimmage, Alabama failed to notice that only ten Georgia players were in formation. The eleventh, flanker Alonzo Awtrey, stood just inside the sideline on the 15-yard line. The Tide didn't pay him any attention because they thought he was the waterboy. Awtrey was dressed in white coveralls and was holding a water bucket.

When the ball was snapped, Awtrey dropped his bucket and sped upfield. Quarterback Timon Bowden fired a pass to Awtrey, who dashed to midfield before he was tackled by a befuddled defender.

Once the Alabama fans realized that their team had been duped, they rushed onto the field to protest, only to be met by the fired-up Georgia spectators. A full-scale riot erupted, and continued until the local police broke up the melee and carted dozens of brawlers off to jail.

Meanwhile, an Alabama official sought out Georgia's acting athletic director, John Morris, and demanded in the name of sportsmanship that the play be called back. When Morris refused, the official flattened him—presumably in the name of sportsmanship.

Feeling somewhat guilty and contrite, Georgia's coach, W.A. Cunningham, who dreamed up the devious play, offered to forget the whole matter and start the game over at the original line of scrimmage. But the officials said there was no rule at the time against the Bulldogs' ruse and they allowed the play to stand. But justice won out: Georgia fumbled three plays later and Alabama recovered. The Bulldogs went on to win, however, 13–9.

At its next meeting, the collegiate rules committee closed the loophole, forcing Georgia to hang up its coveralls for good.

NOTRE DAME "FAINTING IRISH"

Nov. 21, 1953

Unbeaten Notre Dame averted a stunning upset at the hands of the Iowa Hawkeyes by resorting to a fraud that worked to perfection not once but twice.

The Hawkeyes fought surprisingly hard and held a 7–0 lead late in the second quarter, but the heavily favored Fighting Irish engineered a long drive down to the Iowa 12-yard line. Out of time-outs and with only a few seconds left in the half, Notre Dame appeared thwarted by the clock.

Suddenly, tackle Frank Varrichione flopped to the ground in a dead faint. The referee called an official's time-out, stopping the clock with just two seconds remaining, while the injured player was carted off the field.

Varrichione was faking. The only real hurt he suffered was the thought that underdog Iowa was winning. His act was a designed play used in crucial situations when the team needed to stop the clock. Notre Dame coach Frank Leahy even had Varrichione run the fake injury play in practice. The first time he rehearsed it, Varrichione clutched his leg, moaned, screamed, and collapsed in true Hollywood fashion. But Leahy thought it had been a bit overdone. "Frank," said Leahy, "I think we'd better make it total unconsciousness."

That's exactly how Varrichione played it in the Iowa game. His fake injury gave Notre Dame time to pull off one more play—a 9-yard touchdown pass. The half ended in a 7–7 tie.

With the gall of a Dublin con man, the Fighting Irish employed the feigned injury play again in the waning seconds of the game.

Trailing 14–7, Notre Dame used up its time-outs in a last-ditch drive that stalled at the Iowa 10-yard line. The clock ticked toward zero when suddenly Irish captain Don Penza and tackle Art Hunter both fell to the ground, seemingly unconscious. (Actually, three other players—including Varrichione, who made an amazing halftime recovery from his "injury" —also hit the turf at the same time. But quarterback Ralph Guglielmi kicked them in the butt and ordered them to get up because no one, not even believers in leprechauns, were going to fall for the Fighting Irish drama involving five injured players.)

Incredibly, the refs bought the two-man act of Penza and Hunter. Given time to regroup because of the official's time-out, Guglielmi tossed a touchdown pass with just 6 seconds remaining. The conversion tied the game—a game that triggered a storm of protests from across the nation.

The NCAA declared the fake injury play, "dishonest, unsportsmanlike, and contrary to the rules." Then it handed down new rules to forbid feigned injuries designed to stop the clock.

The fraud tarnished Notre Dame's image. In fact, Leahy's boys were called the "Fainting Irish." They were further stung by the college football ratings. Because of the tainted tie, Notre Dame tumbled from the top to No. 2 and remained there the rest of the season, even though their unbeaten record was better than No. 1 Maryland.

All this provided little solace to Iowa fans, who could do nothing more than scream bloody murder over being cheated out of a victory.

Borrowing a few lines from Grantland Rice, Iowa coach Forest Evashevski told fans: "When that one great scorer comes to write against your name/ He writes not that you won or lost/ But how come we got gypped at Notre Dame???"

IOWA HAWKEYES

Nov. 8, 1914

With the game all but won, the Iowa Hawkeyes set out to humiliate the Northwestern Wildcats by suckering them with a sneaky scam—the penalty trick.

During the first half of the game, won by Iowa 27–0, Hawkeye quarterback Sammy Gross deliberately complained to officials time and again about alleged violations perpetrated by Northwestern's defensive line. The irritated Wildcats told Gross to shut up and called him a crybaby.

That's exactly how Gross wanted his opponents to react. He was setting them up for his flimflam.

Late in the fourth quarter, Gross brought his team up to the line of scrimmage on his own 16-yard line. Then he turned to the referee and asked that a penalty be imposed on the opposing defensive left end for holding on the previous play. The innocent end vociferously denied any guilt. The ref, losing patience with the carping Gross, shouted, "Play ball!"

Gross walked up to his center, Max Houghton, and said, "Give me the ball. I'll walk off the penalty myself."

Houghton shook his head and said, "You can't get away with that, Sammy. It's your own funeral, and you'll be kicked out of the game." Nevertheless, the center snapped the ball back to Gross, thus putting the ball in play. With the pigskin tucked under his arm, Gross walked past the line of scrimmage and started to pace off the penalty toward the Wildcats' goal. He shoved Northwestern's defensive back Rollin Gray aside, saying, "Get out of my way."

"Goodbye, Sammy. They'll throw you out of the game for that!" shouted Gray, not realizing the ball was in play. Gross took several more steps, then broke for the open and ran 54 yards before Gray brought him down.

Iowa had pulled off the same play a year earlier against Nebraska. The only difference was that Gross had run only 15 yards before he was tackled—by the referee, who smelled something fishy and put a stop to the phony penalty trick.

CARLISLE INDUSTRIAL SCHOOL INDIANS

Oct. 31, 1903

The crafty Carlisle Indians, who loved nothing better than to win through chicanery, pulled off their greatest trick play ever when they outsmarted the whizzes at Harvard.

But at first it looked like it was Harvard who had outwitted Carlisle.

A week before the Indians-Crimson game, Carlisle used one of coach Pop Warner's dirty tricks in the game against Syracuse. Every time the Indian center snapped the ball, every member of the Carlisle team seemed to be running with it. That's because Warner had sewn patches resembling footballs on the jerseys of all his players!

A Harvard alumnus who saw the game warned Crimson coach Percy Haughton to be on the lookout for the scheme the following week. When the Indians arrived for their game against Harvard, Haughton asked Warner to remove the football patches from the jerseys. But Warner said there was nothing in the rules outlawing them.

Haughton then directed his manager to bring out the footballs that were to be used in the game. To Warner's surprise, every game ball had been painted crimson, matching the color of the Harvard jerseys. "You can't do that!" complained Warner. But Haughton just smiled and said, "There's nothing in the rules outlawing them." So both coaches agreed to use a regulation ball, and the football patches were removed from the Indians' jerseys.

Although Warner was foiled, he still had another dastardly trick up his sleeve. He waited until the start of the second half to spring it on Harvard. He ordered his team to use the "hidden ball" or "hunchback" play.

The kickoff was fielded by quarterback Jimmie Johnson on the 5-yard line. Instead of blocking for him, the rest of the Indians gathered around Johnson. With this huddle as a shield, Johnson deftly and quickly shoved the ball inside the back of guard Charlie Dillon's jersey, which had an elastic band around the bottom to keep the ball from falling out.

Once the ball was secured, Johnson yelled, "Go!" The Indians fanned out in a long line across the field and bounded like antelopes toward the Harvard goal. Each Carlisle back yanked off his leather helmet and hugged it to his chest pretending it was the football to further fake out the Harvard players.

The Indian backs were chased and slammed to the ground, but when the tacklers discovered only headgear and not the football, they began jumping around, yelping like hounds thrown off the scent.

None of the Crimson paid any attention to Carlisle's 6-foot guard, Dillon, who was running with both arms free. Posing as a blocker, Dillon headed straight for Harvard's last defender, safety Carl Marshall. When he saw Dillon bearing down on him, Marshall sidestepped him, thinking Dillon was attempting to block. Then the duped Marshall dashed up the field to join the rest of his bewildered teammates in a frantic search for the football.

Meanwhile, the fans in the grandstands could see the ball bobbing around under Dillon's jersey. A rumble of astonishment turned into a roar of laughter as the spectators pointed at the strange hump on Dillon's back.

But the Harvard players were still scurrying wildly around when

Dillon loped across the goal line. He pulled the ball out from under his jersey, placed it on the ground, and sat on it while Pop Warner chortled with glee on the bench.

Unfortunately for the tricksters, the Crimson enjoyed the last laugh. Harvard beat Carlisle 12–11.

RON MEYER

Coach • New England Patriots • Dec. 12, 1982

Patriots coach Ron Meyer wanted to steal a game, so he did the obvious thing. He called for a burglar.

Convicted burglar Mark Henderson stepped forward, and literally pulled a clever snow job on the Miami Dolphins, leaving them 3–0 losers to New England.

Meyer buried the spirit of fair play during a blinding blizzard in Foxboro, Massachusetts, where the Dolphins and Patriots were locked in a scoreless standstill. Because of the snowstorm, neither team had even remotely threatened to score a touchdown. Each attempted a field goal that failed because of the inclement weather.

However, with 4:45 remaining, New England ground out a drive that stalled out at the Miami 16-yard line. The Patriots then called time to let kicker John Smith clear away a spot on the slick, snow-covered field for a crucial field goal attempt that could win the game.

Suddenly, a light bulb lit up in Coach Meyer's sneaky mind. "I saw John Smith on his hands and knees trying to get the snow cleared, and all of a sudden it hit me," recalled Meyer. "Why not send a snow plow out there?"

He raced down the sideline looking for the operator of the John

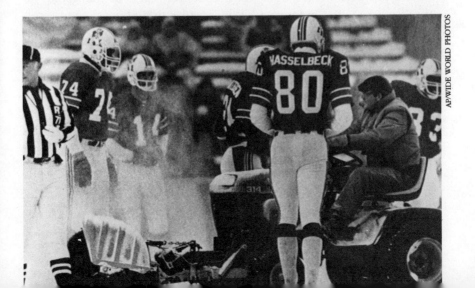

Deere snow plow that had been clearing the yard lines during time-outs. The operator happened to be Mark Henderson, 24, who was serving a 15-year sentence for burglary at Norfolk State Prison and was on the Schaefer Stadium maintenance crew as part of a work-release program. Meyer told Henderson to clear off a spot on the field for Smith.

As you might expect of a person with his address, Henderson jumped when the command was given. He made a beautiful initial fake with the snow plow by retracing his previous path along the 20-yard line. Then, catching officials and Dolphins off guard, he swerved to his left, sweeping snow ahead of him and leaving a perfect swath of green SuperTurf between the 23- and 25-yard lines. It was the best sweep the Patriots fans had seen in years.

The Dolphins cursed and threatened Henderson. But no one stopped him. Explained defensive tackle Bob Baumhower, "I saw him coming, but what was I supposed to do? No way I'm going to take on a plow."

When play resumed, Smith planted his foot squarely in the path cleared by Henderson and kicked a game-winning 33-yard field goal.

The Dolphins cried foul, insisting the snow plow play was illegal. But the term "illegal" meant something quite different to the team than it did to Henderson, the convicted burglar. "What were they gonna do?" he said afterward. "Put me in jail?"

CORNELL BIG RED

Oct. 9, 1965

To defend against a field goal kicker, the Cornell Big Red literally rose to the occasion—and stooped to a new low.

Cornell was battling Princeton when the Tigers marched to the Big Red 19-yard line before their drive sputtered early in the game. So Princeton's soccer-style kicker Charlie Gogolak trotted onto the gridiron to attempt a field goal.

As the Tigers broke their huddle and lined up for the kick, they couldn't believe their eyes. Cornell had built two human towers. Defensive backs Jim Docherty and Dale Witwer climbed onto the shoulders of 6-foot, 5-inch tackles Reeve Vanneman and Harry Garman.

"I thought they were just joking around," Gogolak said later. "It was like a bad dream. I would have liked to hit one of those guys in the head. I'll bet they were up there praying they wouldn't be hit."

As he got ready for the snap, Gogolak noticed that the towers were

ROBERT P. MATTHEWS

not lined up evenly with the goal posts. By aiming his kick slightly to the left, he figured, he could still make the field goal.

Unfortunately for Gogolak, he aimed the ball a little too far to the left and missed the field goal. Unfortunately for Cornell, it didn't matter. The Big Red was penalized 5 yards for being offside. The penalty gave the Tigers a first down, allowing them to complete the touchdown drive.

The tower scheme crumbled after Gogolak booted field goals of 44 and 54 yards over the stacked defense, and Princeton won 36–27. After the season, the Rules Committee condemned the twin towers.

NOTRE DAME MARCHING BAND

Nov. 23, 1935

When Notre Dame engaged in a heated battle against their arch enemies, the University of Southern California Trojans, the Irish marching
band became unabashedly cold and calculating.

The band numbed USC in the 1935 game in South Bend, Indiana.
Despite playing in the coldest weather the Trojans had ever experienced—
the wind chill factor was below zero—USC carried a 6–0 lead into
halftime. But soon the desperate Irish received a little help from the
school band.

The band waited until the Trojans returned to the field and the bitter
cold after halftime. Then, before the team could reach its bench, the
band began playing "Ave Maria" in memory of Joe Sullivan, captain-elect
of the 1935 Irish team, who had died before the season started.

Out of respect, the Trojans stood at attention, shivering as the icy wind
blasted their tanned skins. When they heard the last cord, the USC
players were ready to run to the bench and get under the blankets.
Suddenly the band struck up the song again, and played it through a
second time. The Trojans were frozen in place. Meanwhile, across the
field, the Notre Dame players were huddled under the warmth of thick
wool blankets.

When the second half finally got under way, the teeth-chattering,
half-frozen Trojans couldn't get thawed out. Eight minutes into the third
quarter, they had given up 2 touchdowns and failed to move the ball.
They lost 20–13.

TACKLING DUMMIES

There's nothing like a clean, crisp tackle that drives a ball carrier into the ground. Fans "ooh" and "aah" over the clothesline tackle, the gang tackle, and the shoulder tackle. But they also boo and jeer the player who makes a stupid tackle that goes against the grain of decent football. For "The Tackiest Tackles Ever Made," The Football Hall of SHAME inducts the following:

LARRY "THE WILD MAN" EISENHAUER

Defensive End • Boston Patriots • Sept., 1961

The cruelest tackle ever seen on TV was made by Larry "The Wild Man" Eisenhauer.

It was captured on film and shown on, of all things, Boston's popular daytime kiddie show, "Boom Town," starring Rex Trailer and his comic sidekick Pablo.

The producers thought it would be a great bit for the show if Pablo—a skinny, middle-aged shrimp—tried out for the Patriots. The team agreed to go along with the gag. So Pablo dressed u, in an old-fashioned football uniform from the Knute Rockne era and joined the Patriots on the practice field.

The script called for a mock scrimmage. Pablo would get the handoff and zigzag his way through the Patriot defense for a touchdown. The producers knew the kids at home would squeal with delight at seeing these great big professional football players running around and falling down as Pablo scampered past them.

The script was sound, but the TV people hadn't considered one important factor—Eisenhauer. He wasn't called "The Wild Man" for nothing. He would get so psyched up before a game that he would punch anything—walls, doors, lockers, even teammates. He once put his helmeted head through a locker-room wall in Buffalo. Another time, in Kansas City, he worked himself into such a frenzy that he flung open a locker-room door and barrelled toward the field, forgetting that he was dressed in nothing more than his helmet.

Unfortunately, the director did not know of Eisenhauer's strange and fierce dedication to football. With the shout of "Action!", the cameras rolled, and Pablo began his funny canter through the Patriot defense. Everything was going smoothly as Pablo scooted down to the 20-yard line past the last defender, who just happened to be Eisenhauer.

Suddenly, the 6-foot, 5-inch, 255-pound Patriot was overcome by his killer instinct. All he saw was an enemy player running for a touchdown, one who had to be stopped. So Eisenhauer leaped to his feet, let out a terrifying roar, and charged after the 5-foot, 3-inch, 110-pound clown.

Poor Pablo. With eyes as big as footballs, Pablo ran for his life, but it was no contest. At about the 5-yard line, Eisenhauer jumped on his back and squashed him. Bellowed Eisenhauer, "Nobody gets across our goal line! Not even a clown!"

Pablo was buried in the turf, gasping for breath. The TV crew rushed to his aid and then turned and chastised Eisenhauer. "I'm kind of ashamed of it now," he said recently. "But I just couldn't stand to see anybody score on us if there was a chance I could stop him. He was slow, so it wasn't any trick catching him. I didn't really hurt him. I just sort of jumped on his back. But what the hell. Why give a guy a free touchdown?"

J.V. KING

Reporter • Oct. 18, 1897

As a reporter covering the game between the Colgate Red Raiders and the Syracuse Orangemen, J.V. King tackled his assignment with too much gusto. He didn't just report the story. He *was* the story.

King could hardly be called an objective reporter. The previous year he had starred on Colgate's football team, and even scored the winning touchdown against Syracuse. After graduating, he joined the staff of a newspaper in Hamilton, New York, home of his alma mater.

Now, as a cub reporter, he was assigned to cover Colgate's home game against Syracuse. Jotting down notes from the sidelines, King watched the two teams battle. Actually, he did more than just watch.

Early in the second half of a tie game, Syracuse ball carrier Haden Patten broke into the clear and was heading for a touchdown. King, a man of noble impulse, decided to save his alma mater in this moment of distress. With notepad in one hand and pencil in the other, he rushed out from the sidelines onto the field. Then, without even the formality of removing his derby hat, he tackled Patten.

Pandemonium erupted as players, officials, and spectators argued over what should be done. The play was upheld, and the game ended in a 6–6 tie. Syracuse vowed to get even. The school refused to play Colgate in any sport for the next five years.

Meanwhile, King's outrageous tackle made big news. Said one local newspaper, "Colgate should get him back in college and on the team where he can make his tackles within the rules of the game and save his good clothes and derby hat."

BOBBY YANDELL

Halfback · Mississippi Rebels · Nov. 29, 1941

No tackle was more stupid than the one made by Bobby Yandell. He brought down his own teammate!

It couldn't have come at a worse time. The Ole Miss Rebels were battling their arch rivals, the Mississippi State Bulldogs, for the Southeastern Conference championship.

In the second quarter of a scoreless tie, the Rebels had the ball on their own 45-yard line when tailback Junior Hovious dropped back to throw a pass to either Yandell or end Ray Poole.

With a neat move, Poole broke free and had his defender beat by a few steps. But Hovious was scrambling for his life in a backfield crowded with onrushing linemen. Seeing Hovious in trouble, Poole put on the brakes and doubled back just as the ball was thrown.

Poole's defender had the bead on the interception, but Poole managed to jump high enough to snare the ball. Meanwhile, Yandell, who was right in front of the play, somehow got himself turned around and became totally confused about who was running where.

Poole twisted free from the grasp of the defender and saw an open field ahead of him. It looked like a sure touchdown. Nobody could stop him now. Nobody but his own teammate. Poole started to take off for the goal line, expecting Yandell to block for him. But Yandell, in his fuzzy-minded bewilderment, tackled him instead at the Bulldog 46-yard line. He had killed the Rebels' big chance to score. Unable to overcome his blunder, Ole Miss failed to keep the drive alive.

The boneheaded tackle proved costly. Without the "sure touchdown," the Rebels lost the game 6–0, and with it, the SEC title.

TOMMY LEWIS

Fullback • Alabama Crimson Tide • Jan. 1, 1954

With one tackle, Tommy Lewis secured his place in football history—and in the annals of shame.

He was too competitive and too emotional for his own good. Lewis leaped off the bench and tackled a touchdown-bound runner, sending the Cotton Bowl in an uproar.

It happened midway into the second period, with the Rice Owls leading the Crimson Tide 7–6. Alabama quarterback Bart Starr fumbled the ball, and it was recovered by the Owls on their own 5-yard line. On the next play, the Owls sprang halfback Dick Moegle, who skirted right end and, with clear sailing ahead, dashed upfield parallel to the sideline.

From the Alabama bench, Lewis, who had been elected team captain for the game, watched in horror. "He's going all the way!" he shouted in alarm. When Moegle reached the 48-yard line—directly in front of Lewis—the super-competitive 'Bama back could no longer contain himself. Lewis gave in to the temptation that has beckoned football players for decades.

Acting on sudden impulse—he didn't even have his helmet on—Lewis charged onto the field at the 44-yard line and tackled Moegle, who tumbled to the 38-yard line. Then Lewis moved sheepishly back to his spot on the sideline. He plopped down on the bench and buried his head in his hands as the startled crowd gasped in amazement.

Immediately after the shocking tackle, the officials decided to award Moegle a touchdown, and he was credited with a 95-yard run. There was no protest from the Alabama bench. Throughout the game, Moegle put on a dazzling performance, racking up 264 yards and leading Rice to a 28–6 victory. But it was Lewis who stole the limelight.

"I'm too emotional," he told reporters after the game. "I kept telling myself, 'I didn't do it. I didn't do it.' But I knew I had." Lewis, who went to the Rice dressing room at halftime to apologize, told the press, "I'm just too full of Alabama."

Strangely, the public didn't cast any blame on Lewis. People hailed him as a "great competitor." He was buried under a mound of sympathetic letters and telegrams and deluged with offers to appear on radio and TV shows and to speak at banquets. Lewis even appeared on "The Ed Sullivan Show," where he received a thunderous ovation.

The public shouldn't have been so kind. Lewis' off-the-bench tackle hurt Alabama more than fans realized. Films show that Moegle would have been tackled just a few yards farther downfield even if Lewis had not come off the bench. That's because the Crimson Tide's speedy back, Bill Oliver, ran a line of pursuit that would have given him a clear shot at shoving Moegle out of bounds at the 35-yard line—three yards from where Lewis beat him to it. The awarded touchdown gave Rice a 14–6 lead and definitely changed the momentum—and eventually the outcome—of the game.

HEADLESS COACHES

The bowl games lost, the plays blown, and the reputations tarnished aren't always due to players' goofs. Sometimes the bungling on the gridiron is the result of bubbleheaded coaching from the sidelines. Too often the head coach takes a nap while the players take the rap. For "The Dumbest Coaching Blunders," The Football Hall of SHAME inducts the following:

BEAR BRYANT

Coach ▪ Kentucky Wildcats ▪ Jan. 1, 1950

Running a practice routine that would have made Marines wince, coach Bear Bryant worked his Kentucky Wildcats to exhaustion. As a result, the tuckered-out team was upset 21–13 by tiny Santa Clara in the Orange Bowl.

Bryant, one of the winningest college coaches of all time, later admitted it was one of the worst coaching mistakes he ever made. "I never really found out the best way to prepare a team for a bowl," he said, "but that game taught me how not to."

Even though Santa Clara (7–2–1) was smaller and weaker than the powerhouse Wildcats (9–2), Bryant took no chances. Two weeks before the game in Miami, the team left wintry Lexington, Kentucky and flew to Cocoa Beach, Florida.

They went straight from the airport to the practice field, where they scrimmaged for more than two hours in the hot, muggy afternoon—until players began passing out. When the field was littered with thirteen victims of heat exhaustion, Bryant showed the sympathy of a sadistic drill sergeant. Turning to trainer Smokey Harper, Bryant said, "Can't you keep them off the field so we can have some room to practice?"

Adding to the players' miseries were painful sandspurs on the field that pierced their skin, sometimes even under their shoulder pads. Nevertheless, with a Foreign Legion mentality, Bryant forced the Wildcats to practice every day from 9:30 A.M. to noon and from 2:30 P.M. to 5 P.M. in full pads. Morning and afternoon practices were followed by skull sessions.

In a brief flash of humanity, Bryant took his team to Miami on Christmas Eve and let them celebrate Christmas Day without a practice. But the following day, he drilled them again with two-a-days right up until game day. "That's the one time he went too far," recalled wide receiver Charlie McClendon. "None of us thought about quitting because it was a bowl game, but he overdid it."

Meanwhile, Santa Clara coach Len Casanova treated his players differently—with kindness. He and his Broncos enjoyed a leisurely four-day train trip from California, stopping along the way to rest and admire the scenery. The Broncos spent only three days in Miami preparing for the game. That's because Casanova heeded the advice of a greyhound trainer who said that if you work greyhounds too hard in Miami, don't expect a good showing out of them. Humans should be treated much the same, the trainer reasoned.

The advice paid off. After gaining a 7–0 halftime lead, the bushed Wildcats faltered and ran out of gas in the second half, losing to the California underdogs.

Bryant, who usually ranted and raved after a loss, was surprisingly subdued. He had no one to blame but himself. In the locker room, he told his team, "Boys, hold your heads up. It's my fault. I just worked you too hard."

FRANK MASON

Coach · Mississippi Rebels · Nov. 28, 1907

Coach Frank Mason devised the dizziest game plan ever for keeping his players' spirits up. He let them tipple whiskey-laced coffee on the sidelines. Not surprisingly, they were plastered—in more ways than one.

Mason brought out the whoopee water for the Ole Miss game against the Mississippi State Bulldogs on a miserable, cold, wet Thanksgiving Day in Jackson. Throughout the contest, the Rebels ran to the sidelines and quaffed gallons of the liquor from a large coffee urn. Officials thought the Ole Miss team was only drinking hot java to take the chill out of their bones.

Actually, the booze fired up the Rebels, who played inspired defense, battling the Bulldogs in a scoreless first half. But in the second half, Ole Miss played like pie-eyed hooch hounds because they *were* pie-eyed hooch hounds. They had the tightest ends and fullest backs in football. The only bottoms up they saw were their own.

The Rebels fumbled balls, muffed punts, and missed tackles, and staggered to a 15–0 loss. (Touchdowns were worth 5 points in those days.) But at least they felt no pain.

After the game, however, the mood of the soused players turned ugly. They blamed their coach for the loss. Mason wasn't too thrilled with them either. Asked by a reporter from the *Daily Clarion-Ledger* if the team was returning home that night, Mason replied, "Yes, the team is going north at 11 o'clock. I'm going in another direction, and hope I never see them again!"

RAY GRAVES

Coach · Florida Gators · Nov. 9, 1968

After racing to a 4–0 record and earning a national ranking, the Florida Gators stumbled and went winless in their next three games. Naturally, the alumni began grumbling. Coach Ray Graves was desperate—and worried. His team faced the undefeated Georgia Bulldogs in their next game.

Graves felt he had to do something. He would have been better off if he had done nothing. In one of the dumbest coaching moves ever, he made his defensive chief, Gene Ellenson, his offensive coach, and his offensive chief, Ed Kensler, his defensive coach.

They reacted the same way cops and robbers or Rebels and Yankees would respond if ordered to switch sides. They felt so strange and out of place they didn't know what to do.

Predictably, the Florida offense played defensively (as in with their backs to the wall) against Georgia, while the defense played offensively (as in pathetic enough to make a preacher swear). The Gators were skinned 51–0, although the game wasn't as close as the score indicated. The Bulldogs ran up a whopping total of 591 yards in total offense compared to Florida's 232 yards.

"It was the worst beating I've ever had either as a player or a coach," lamented Ellenson. "This game, and life in general, seems to work that way. When things start going bad, they go in bunches." Like in bananas—which accurately describes Graves' coaching move.

ED JONTOS

Coach • Rensselaer Poly Institute Engineers • Oct. 4, 1947

Coach Ed Jontos could have kicked himself for losing a game that his Engineers seemed a shoo-in to win.

Rensselaer Poly was beating the University of Buffalo 7–0 in the third quarter when Jontos' star player, defensive end Stan Gorzelnic, came to the sidelines. He pointed to his left shoe, which was badly ripped.

Because the school ran the football program on a limited budget, the team didn't have any spare shoes. So Jontos did the next best thing. He searched up and down the bench for a replacement shoe that would fit Gorzelnic's size 13 foot.

"Who wears a size 13?" Jontos asked his benchwarmers. No one said a word. "Take off your shoes," he barked. "You don't know what size you're wearing anyway."

Jontos checked one shoe after another, but it was no use. There wasn't a size 13 among them. Meanwhile, without Gorzelnic at defensive end, Buffalo scored two touchdowns by running the ball right at—and through—his hapless substitute.

Jontos was beside himself with anger. Eventually, the team trainer performed a crude repair job on the battered shoe and Gorzelnic returned to the game. But it was too late. The Engineers lost 14–7.

In the losers' locker room, the players were somberly undressing when Jontos shouted, "We lost the game because of a shoe!" With that said, he yanked off one of his shoes and flung it, narrowly missing one of his linemen. The player picked up the shoe and casually glanced inside. It was none other than a size 13.

HUNK ANDERSON

Coach • Notre Dame Fighting Irish • Nov. 21, 1931

Unbeaten Notre Dame was winning 14–0 over its arch rival, the University of Southern California, as the fourth quarter began. Rather than play it safe with his starters, Fighting Irish coach Hunk Anderson went in for the kill. He sent in fresh troops, the eager second stringers. His move proved to be the deathblow, all right—for Notre Dame.

The subs showed the crowd of 50,731 just why they were second stringers. They were totally inept. On offense they couldn't move the ball, and on defense they couldn't stop the resurging Trojans.

There wasn't anything Anderson could do about it, either. In those days, the rules prevented a player from entering the lineup more than once in each period. With his regulars sitting glumly on the bench, Anderson watched victory slip from his grasp as the Trojans racked up 16 unanswered points in the fourth quarter to win 16–14.

Anderson's classic blunder not only cost his team victory but also brought a crushing end to Notre Dame's 26-game unbeaten streak. Fighting Irish fans never forgave him.

SNOOZE PLAYS

Coaches and players commit to memory every detail of the game plan and the playbook. Baloney! These guys daydream and forget things just like the rest of us working stiffs. The only problem is that their office is the playing field, and when they get caught napping, they're in for a rude awakening. For "The Most Mind-Boggling Mental Miscues," The Football Hall of SHAME inducts the following:

FRANCIS SCHMIDT

Coach • Tulsa–Arkansas–Texas Christian–Ohio State–Idaho • 1919–42

No coach was more absentminded than Francis Schmidt.

His attention was locked on football 24 hours a day, seven days a week. He didn't just daydream about the game, he weekdreamed it. Every neuron of his brain was occupied with X's and O's.

Schmidt was even more absorbed with football than was his forgetful peer Howard Jones, coach of the University of Southern California from 1925–40. Jones' mind was centered so deeply on the game that he ignored traffic signals, misplaced keys, stranded family members, missed appointments, and even forgot his way home. But Jones couldn't top Schmidt when it came to absentmindedness.

Schmidt would stamp a letter and sit on it to be sure the stamp stuck. Then he would forget where the letter was. Raging and swearing, Schmidt would scatter the papers on his desk in a futile search. Finally someone would summon up the nerve to tell him he was sitting on it. "Well," Schmidt would growl, "why in the hell didn't you tell me sooner?"

Schmidt's forgetfulness caused him much pain on the sidelines. In 1927, when he was coach at Arkansas, carpenters completed a shelter over the Razorback bench just before a game against Oklahoma State. Midway through the game, a pass went through the outstretched arms of an Arkansas defender and into the hands of an Oklahoma State receiver for a touchdown. Schmidt was so upset he leaped off the bench and, forgetting about the newly built structure, struck his head against the shelter and knocked himself out cold.

He also wiped himself out in a tense game in 1931 when he was coach at Texas Christian. Enraged by a penalty against his team, Schmidt charged out onto the field. The only problem was that he forgot to take off the headphones he used to talk with his assistant in the press box. When Schmidt reached the end of the wire, it flipped him over. He lay on his back cursing the wire, the phone, and the hapless, red-eared assistant on the other end.

A few years later, when Schmidt took over the head coaching job at Ohio State, he and an assistant left on a recruiting trip. They stopped for gas and the assistant went into the cafe next door. Schmidt stayed in the car, making notes. Once the tank was filled and he had paid for the gas, Schmidt drove on, completely forgetting about the assistant he was leaving behind.

Another time, Schmidt drove his car into a filling station in Columbus to have the oil changed. He stayed behind the wheel, drawing plays in a notebook while the car was raised on a hoist.

Oblivious to the world around him, the coach pored over his diagrams. In a few minutes he came up with a play that looked unstoppable. With a small cry of triumph, he slapped the notebook shut, opened the door, stepped out—and fell ten feet to the concrete below.

JOHNNY BLOOD

Coach ▪ Pittsburgh Steelers ▪ Nov. 20, 1938

It's customary for a coach to worry about his players. In Pittsburgh, however, it was also customary for the players to worry about their coach, Johnny Blood.

Because he had a reputation as a hellraiser off the field, the team just couldn't depend on him to show up.

After playing an exhibition game in Los Angeles, the Steelers headed home on the train—one that Blood missed. When he failed to show up for practice the following week, the team grew concerned, although not alarmed. After all, he was a lousy coach. In his short two-year career as head coach, Blood was able to win only 6 of 25 games.

The following Sunday, Blood was spotted at Wrigley Field watching the Chicago Bears play the Green Bay Packers. Perplexed sportswriters strolled up to Blood and asked him why he wasn't with his team.

"Oh, we're not playing this week," he explained.

No sooner did he get those words out of his mouth than the public address announcer gave a final score: Philadelphia 14, Pittsburgh 7.

HERBERT HOOVER

Manager ▪ Stanford Cardinals ▪ March 19, 1892

Herbert Hoover, later to become President of the United States, organized Stanford's football team and set up its first big game—one that almost didn't happen because he forgot one minor detail.

As team manager, Hoover had had 15,000 tickets printed up for the contest against arch rival California. The game attracted such a huge crowd that Hoover ran out of tickets by early afternoon. At the admission gate, he was forced to collect coins in empty washtubs, boxes, and anything else he could scrounge up.

As the 3 P.M. kickoff time approached, the 20,000 banner-waving, cheer-shouting fans tingled with excitement over the impending start of what promised to be a long and fierce football rivalry.

The teams were pumped up for action and roared their approval when referee Jack Sherrard signaled them to get ready. Then he asked Hoover for the game ball.

Hoover's jaw dropped. He had arranged for most everything—tickets,

the concessions, the security, and the stadium—but he plum forgot to bring a football!

While the crowd moaned and fidgeted, David Goulcher, owner of a sporting goods store in downtown San Francisco, hopped on his horse and galloped into town for a ball. He returned an hour later. The players' cheers turned to groans when they discovered that Goulcher hadn't brought a regulation football. Instead, the teams had to play the delayed game (won by Stanford 14–10) with an inflated bladder.

CLARENCE HERSCHBERGER

Halfback • University of Chicago Maroons • Nov. 13, 1897

It was the night before the big game against Wisconsin. A victory over the Badgers would give the favored, unbeaten Chicago Maroons their first conference title.

But it was not to be—because Clarence Herschberger, the star of the Maroons, forgot the training table rules.

Herschberger was a slick runner with swivel hips, a key man both offensively and defensively. But his greatest asset to the team was his golden toe, which kicked the Maroons to victory after victory.

One of the reasons for the team's success was that the players adhered

48

to training rules and stayed in shape with a proper diet. On the eve of the Wisconsin game, Herschberger told Walter Kennedy, the team captain and quarterback, "I'll sure be glad when this season is over. I'm going to eat my way through a whole steer."

"You could never do it," retorted Kennedy. "I can out-eat you any day of the week."

Never one to back down from a challenge, Herschberger said, "Those Badgers are big and we need all the weight we can muster against them. Tell you what. I bet I can put on more weight than you between now and game time."

"You're on!" said Kennedy.

The pair stripped and carefully weighed in. Then, despite orders to stick to a strict diet to keep lean and mean, the two gorged themselves at the training table like pigs at the trough. Stuffed to the gills, they waddled over to the scales. Herschberger had gained seven pounds but Kennedy had tacked on a quarter pound more.

Piqued by this setback, Herschberger declared, "I'll out-weigh you by game time."

At least Kennedy knew when to stop; he would have no more of this culinary contest. After all, they had a football game to play. Herschberger, however, was determined to win the bet and the next morning, just hours before kickoff, he wolfed down thirteen large eggs.

By game time he had the look of a week-old omelet and felt just as rotten. Suffering from a severe case of gastritis, Herschberger was lost for the whole game. Without their star, the Maroons were clobbered 23–8, their only defeat in 12 starts. Also lost was their bid for the championship of the Western Athletic Conference (later known as the Big Ten).

Complained coach Amos Alonzo Stagg, "We weren't beaten by eleven Badgers. We were beaten by thirteen eggs!"

ST. LOUIS CARDINALS

Oct. 16, 1966

While setting up for a crucial punt return, the St. Louis Cardinals left their brains at the line of scrimmage, bringing shame to the name of special teams everywhere.

Only 1:48 remained in a 10–10 game against the visiting Dallas Cowboys, who were faced with fourth-and-five at their own 49-yard line.

Danny Villanueva of the Cowboys stood back in punt formation and the ball was snapped. But the Cardinals didn't charge Villanueva to block the ball, or even to harass the punter. In fact, not a single Cardinal crossed the line of scrimmage.

Incredibly, they all turned their backs to Villanueva and ran downfield to form a picket line for punt returner Johnny Roland, who was waiting for the ball on the St. Louis 20-yard line. They were hoping to spring for a long return. But they forgot one important element—the punter.

Villanueva took one step forward, stopped, and couldn't believe his eyes. He saw nothing but a wall of St. Louis jerseys all moving away from him. Villanueva, who hadn't run from punt formation since high school, began to scamper downfield.

He ran past the line of scrimmage, then past the first down marker right in front of the St. Louis bench. Cardinal coach Charley Winner was going bananas. Although he stayed off the field, Winner ran alongside Villanueva swearing at him and screaming at the top of his lungs to his unmindful players, "Hey, you stupid bastards, turn around! Turn around!" But none of the oblivious Cardinals did.

Finally, after yelling in earthier language, Winner caught the attention of St. Louis defender Roy Shivers. He was the first to wake up from the team's mental slumber, and knocked Villanueva out of bounds at the St. Louis 28-yard line.

It would have served the Cardinals right if they had lost the game on that play. As it turned out, Villanueva's easy 23-yard gain set up his own attempt at a 33-yard field goal that would have won the game with just 31 seconds remaining. But Villanueva's kick was short and to the left. The game ended in a tie.

ROY "WRONG WAY" RIEGELS

Center • California Golden Bears • Jan. 1, 1929

Roy Riegels has etched his name in college football history as the No. 1 bonehead of all time.

He forgot which way to run!

In a span of about 10 seconds, Riegels cost his school the victory in the 1929 Rose Bowl, made himself a legend among bumblers, and earned a new nickname—"Wrong Way."

It all began in the second quarter of a scoreless tie between his team, the California Golden Bears, and the Georgia Tech Yellow Jackets.

Tech running back Stumpy Thomason was hit on his own 36-yard line and fumbled. The ball bounced to the Tech 40 with both teams in hot pursuit. During the wild scramble for the loose ball, Riegels, the California center, picked it out of the air. He started running downfield in the right direction and was only 30 yards away from a go-ahead touchdown when suddenly his radar went awry. While pivoting to get away from a tackler, Riegels completely lost his bearings. He wheeled around in a U-turn and legged it out for all he was worth toward his *own* end zone.

Centers aren't supposed to be fast runners. But Riegels was sprinting like a man possessed, pumped up with the determination of which heroes are made. Some of his teammates were fooled by his misguided attempt at glory and they began knocking down Georgia Tech tacklers who themselves seemed confused.

The legendary sports broadcaster Graham McNamee, who was calling the play-by-play on radio, couldn't believe his eyes. "What's the matter with me?" he shouted into the microphone. "Am I going crazy?"

Tech players on the bench jumped up and began to shout, but coach Bill Alexander ordered them to sit down. "He's running the wrong way," the coach said. "Let's see how far he can go."

Riegels would have gone all the way if it hadn't been for the clear thinking of Benny Lom, the California quarterback. Lom immediately

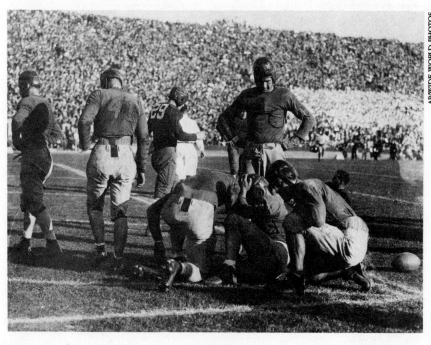

chased his teammate, shouting, "Stop, Roy! You're going the wrong way!" At the 10-yard line, Lom caught Riegels and slowed him down with a bear hug, but Riegels shook him off. "Get away from me!" shrieked Riegels. "This is my touchdown!" At the 3-yard line, Lom grabbed him again and this time held on. Riegels finally realized that something was wrong and turned around. Just then a wave of Georgia Tech players smeared him on the 1-yard line.

Riegels had run nearly 70 yards in the wrong direction! He sat on the ground in shock as his sympathetic teammates came over and consoled him. They had always looked up to him; in fact, before the game, they had voted him captain for the following season.

California decided the best way to get out of this jam—as well as get Riegels off the hook—was to punt. But Lom's punt from the end zone was blocked for a safety. It was the most crucial play of the game because the safety gave the Yellow Jackets the 2 points they needed for an eventual 8–7 victory.

After the safety, a dejected Riegels trudged to the sidelines and took himself out of the game. But after listening to the entreaties of his teammates, he played the entire second half.

Eventually, the Rules Committee passed a rule prohibiting an opponent from advancing a fumble that strikes the ground. But the rule change couldn't erase the shame of Riegels' wrong-way run.

NEW YORK JETS

Jan. 13, 1969

Every year, pro football teams strive for one goal—winning the Super Bowl. Nothing is more important than carting home that dazzling trophy—a cherished, sought-after symbol declaring its holders the best team in the world.

Throughout the 1968 season, the brash, upstart New York Jets, led by Broadway Joe Namath, coveted that trophy. They wanted it and they were determined to win it.

Representing the AFL at Super Bowl III in Miami, the Jets were 18-point underdogs against the Baltimore Colts. But Namath, his heart set on capturing the trophy, declared, "The Jets will win on Sunday, I guarantee it." Namath was true to his word. In a stunning upset that shocked the sports world, the Jets whomped the Colts 16–7 to win the Super Bowl.

The trophy was theirs. In all its gleaming glory, the 21-inch sterling silver championship trophy signified that the Jets were No. 1. Just wait, said the team, until the fans back in New York see this. Unfortunately for the fans, that's exactly what they had to do: wait. Incredibly, when the Jets flew home the day after their Super Bowl triumph, they forgot the very thing they had worked so hard to get—the trophy!

"That wasn't exactly our finest hour, especially coming right after our finest game," admitted Frank Ramos, the Jets public relations director. "After all the celebrating that went on, I don't think anybody was in any condition to think about things like who had the trophy. Some of the guys had enough trouble just finding the airport.

"On the flight back to New York, it was one of those 'Who's got the trophy?' 'Do you have the trophy?' 'Where is the trophy?'

"When we got back home, a big crowd was waiting. It sure was embarrassing when all those fans asked to see the trophy we'd won and we didn't have anything to show them."

So where was the trophy? An assistant found it back at the team's Fort Lauderdale hotel, next to a bunch of left-behind equipment.

THE MEAN TEAM

Some players are just plain mean. They play as though they left their consciences on the sidelines. Their actions on and off the gridiron are so heartless that they make Rambo look like a wimp. They don't walk around with chips on their shoulder pads—they carry two-by-fours. Maybe they aren't so bad once you get to know them . . . but why bother? For "The Meanest Players of All Time," The Football Hall of SHAME inducts the following:

CONRAD DOBLER

Guard • St. Louis Cardinals–New Orleans Saints–Buffalo Bills • 1972–81

Meanness poured out of Conrad Dobler like sweat.

As the NFL's No. 1 villain throughout the 1970s, Dobler could do it all—bite fingers, gouge eyes, kick shins, grab face masks. He didn't specialize.

AP/WIDE WORLD PHOTOS

The 6-foot, 3-inch, 255-pound offensive guard actually enjoyed his reputation of being mean enough to shove little old ladies out into the street for laughs. In fact, he went out of his way to make sure that the world knew Genghis Khan was alive and well and playing football under the name of Conrad Dobler.

Accused of clawing at the flesh behind opponents' face masks, he told reporters, "My hand at times has possibly slipped under the face masks." Sometimes Dobler's hands slipped all the way up to his opponents' eyes. "I wouldn't try to blind someone," he once said. "Maybe blur their vision." He explained that the reason he kept hitting players long after the whistle had blown was because "my timing may have been off a little." As for charges that he deliberately chewed on opponents' fingers, Dobler claimed that he never "knowingly" bit another player because he had a high regard for oral hygiene.

Dobler's meanness peaked in 1974 when he played for the St. Louis Cardinals. Because he had broken his left hand, he wore a fingertip-to-elbow plaster cast for much of the season, and used it like a club. "I was sticking it (the cast) out there, and they just happened to run right into it," he claimed. "The most effective place to use it is the throat. It really makes a guy stop short." Before one early-season game, Philadelphia Eagles linebacker Bill Bergey demanded to inspect the rock-hard cast. Dobler told him to look at it real close. When Bergey bent down, Dobler raised his arm up and smashed Bergey in the mouth.

In another game, Dobler punched Oakland Raiders linebacker Phil Villapiano right in the ribs. Later, Dobler told Villapiano, "The only reason I did it was that I knew your ribs were injured."

Dobler threw his cheapest shot of the year at Dallas Cowboys defensive back Cliff Harris. Groggy and hurt from a block, Harris was slowly pulling himself up to his knees. "I was about 20 yards away," recalled Dobler. "But I thought, 'Why not? What the hell!' I hit him alongside the earlobe and his head bounced three or four times." They carried Harris off the field on a stretcher.

Dobler went to even greater lengths to show off his savagery. When he noticed that Eagles safety Bill Bradley was sprawled out on the field after an injury, Dobler lumbered nearly 50 yards just to spit in Bradley's face.

After playing opposite Dobler in the final game of the regular season in 1974, New York Giants rookie defensive tackle Jim Pietrzak was foolish enough to attempt a brief, friendly chat with Dobler. "I went up to Dobler and wished him good luck in the play-offs," recalled Pietrzak. "He turned around and punched me in the throat."

In the play-offs, Dobler mercilessly worked over Doug Sutherland, the

Minnesota Vikings' young defensive tackle. Limping off the field after a ball exchange in the second quarter, Sutherland demanded a pair of baseball catcher's shinguards from the equipment man. "I'm not going to get through this game without some special protection," said Sutherland. "Dobler has kicked me square in the shins five times, tackled me around the knees twice and bitten me once." At halftime, Sutherland and another Viking asked the team physician for rabies shots because Dobler was biting them. "I never played a football game before where I also had to worry about rabies," Sutherland lamented.

The following year, 1975, a national TV audience saw firsthand just how mean and nasty Dobler could play. On a Monday night football game between the Washington Redskins and the St. Louis Cardinals, an isolated camera focused on Dobler as he matched up against tackle Bill Brundige. The replay clearly showed that Dobler had illegally grabbed Brundige, made him stumble, and booted him in the shins. "There you have it, folks," said sportscaster Alex Karras. "Holding, tripping, kicking. All on the *same* play. That's Conrad Dobler, the dirtiest player in professional football."

Dobler took exception to that label. "I like to think I'm an innovative player," he said. "I do things differently than most other guards."

One unnamed player summed up Dobler's mean streak this way: "What you need for Dobler is a string of garlic buds around your neck and an iron stake. If they played every game under a full moon, Dobler would make All-Pro. He must be the only guy in the league who sleeps in a casket."

ROGER "ZANY" ZATKOFF

Tackle–Linebacker · Green Bay Packers–Detroit Lions · 1953–58

When the Detroit Lions acquired Zany Zatkoff from the Green Bay Packers in 1957, the Lions were delighted. Before the season was over, though, they wondered if Zany was still on the Packer payroll.

He was so ferocious that he sidelined, at one time or another, all three of his team's regular defensive backs. That's because he hit with ruthless abandon anybody who got between him and the ball. Zany was an equal oppurtunity annihilator; he maimed victims without regard to race, creed, or color of jersey. "That was my philosophy on football," Zany recalled. "And sometimes it meant wiping out my own teammates. That seemed to irritate them for some reason."

Teammate Joe Schmidt, Detroit's middle linebacker, finally discovered the secret to staying alive while playing on the same side with Zatkoff. Schmidt would look for Zany first before going after the ball carrier.

But Zatkoff's brutality was so unsettling to the rest of his teammates that they decided not to take any chances, especially during practice. One day Detroit quarterback Bobby Layne called Zany to the center of the practice field while the rest of the team surrounded him.

"We don't want anybody to get hurt," Layne told Zatkoff, "and therefore we want to keep our eye on you at all times. And if we can't see you, at least we want to be able to hear you." With that said, the players tied a set of cowbells on Zany and made him wear them during practice scrimmages. It was the NFL's first Distant Early Warning System.

Zany gave opponents plenty to think about—their insurance premiums, for instance. He didn't just tackle runners; he speared them. Although spearing is outlawed today, back then Zatkoff was allowed to mangle runners by lowering his head and trying to ram his helmet through their chests. His teammates thought he was crazy for tackling with his head so they tagged him with the nickname Zany.

"My goal was always to see how many guys I could take out at one time during a kickoff," said Zany. "I could always get two, that was easy. By giving up my body, I once got three. But I never did take out four—although I sure tried. But what the hell, it sure did my heart good to see them carry off the field two players that I'd put out with one whack."

Zatkoff took fiendish pleasure in belting quarterbacks so viciously they ended up in the Twilight Zone. No hit was more satisfying to Zany than the devastating blow he dealt to Baltimore Colts star Johnny Unitas. The quarterback collapsed in a heap. A few seconds later, the woozy Unitas tried to stagger to his feet. Rather than help, Zatkoff stood over him, laughed, and said, "I really got in a good lick, didn't I?"

Meanwhile, Zatkoff's teammate Joe Schmidt—a tough player in his own right, but one who's heart still beat—saw that Unitas was on the verge of losing consciousness. The concerned Schmidt told Unitas to sit back down on the ground whereupon Zany turned to his teammate and snarled, "Let the son of a bitch fall!"

DICK BUTKUS

Linebacker • Chicago Bears • 1965–73

In a game known for its savagery, Dick Butkus was the most blood-thirsty, anti-social, frothing-at-the-mouth monster of mayhem ever to terrorize the gridiron.

Every autumn he led the league in the administration of concussions and contusions that still hurt in the spring. Butkus left his mark on everyone he hit, with an elbow to the ribs, a knee in the groin, or teeth on an arm.

The 6-foot, 3-inch, 245-pound sadistic linebacker's presence alone was enough to scare running backs out of their Adidas lowcuts. Said Butkus in all candor, "I wouldn't ever want to hurt anybody deliberately, unless it was important—like a league game or something."

He was a man-eating grizzly on the loose. Typical of his play was his performance in a 1969 game against the Detroit Lions. After smothering end Charlie Sanders in a gut-wrenching bear hug, Butkus poked his fingers through Sanders' face mask trying to scratch out his eyes. The next day, Lions general manager Russ Thomas declared, "Something has to be done about Butkus. He's too vicious, too brutal. He goes beyond the rules."

There were no rules at the School of Destruction where Butkus earned a doctorate. For his Ph.D. dissertation, he tried to break the ankle of Green Bay running back MacArthur Lane. "Butkus just grabbed the lower part of my leg and tried to crack it in half over his knee," Lane recalled. "It was like you'd break up kindling for a fire. He didn't break it. I guess my leg was too green."

During his playing days, O.J. Simpson once said of Butkus, "He doesn't want to hurt you. He wants to kill you."

Before each play, Butkus, a direct descendant of Frankenstein's monster, glowered at the opposing quarterback with bulging, hate-filled eyes. Growling with bloodcurdling menace, he hurled horrific insults at the opponent's backfield that would have made a drill sergeant wince.

Whenever Butkus broke up a play, it wasn't so much a tackle as a demonstration of what havoc a human can wreak. He loved to tear apart the enemy. Perhaps that explains why, in describing a favorite movie scene, he said, "A head was cut off and it went rolling down the stairs and I sort of liked that."

Butkus feared no one. Once, in a game against the St. Louis Cardinals, he stormed over to the opposing team's bench and shouted at the players, "You're nothing but a bunch of no-good sons of bitches!" Not a single player so much as uttered a word back.

Butkus hated referees as much as opponents. During one game, the NFL's meanest linebacker was heading toward the Bears' defensive huddle and an official happened to be in the way. By swerving slightly, Butkus could have avoided the ref. Butkus didn't swerve. He "accidentally" decked the official with an elbow and sent him reeling for a 5-yard loss.

In a 1969 exhibition game in Miami, Butkus was ejected after biting an official. Trying to break up a brawl started by Butkus, referee Ralph Morcroft ended up at the bottom of a big pile of fighting players. Morcroft grabbed Butkus' face mask to keep him from getting up. But one of Morcroft's fingers went in too far behind the face mask—so Butkus bit it to the bone. Wrote a Miami sportswriter, "Either Butkus is carnivorous or the Bears are just not setting out the right kind of pre-game meal."

HARDY BROWN

Linebacker • Baltimore Colts–Washington Redskins–San Francisco 49ers– Chicago Cardinals • 1950–56

Hardy Brown was a former Marine paratrooper who played football one way—to the death. Opponents' cries of pain were music to his ears. Hardy believed football was invented by a mean SOB, so he played the game like one.

He didn't just tackle ball carriers. He maimed them. Playing in the days before face masks, Brown would spring up at his opponent and blast him under the chin with a numbing, vicious blow from the shoulder. Brown knocked out more men and broke more jaws than did Joe Louis. Thank God, Brown was small for his position, at 6-feet, 195 pounds. If he'd been any bigger, he'd be serving time for manslaughter.

Most of the mayhem he committed came in the early 1950s when he was a member of the San Francisco 49ers. Brown never left his heart in San Francisco simply because he didn't have one. He was so ruthless and savage that his own teammates wouldn't let him scrimmage in intra-squad games. But it was that same barbarity that appealed to a strange group of 49er fans—a coterie of sadists who came to the games solely to see Brown flatten ball carriers with his lethal shoulder tackle. Often, opponents would ask officials to conduct a pre-game inspection of Hardy's shoulder pads for metal reinforcements. The refs never found any. Brown wasn't dirty. He was just mean.

Hardy's greatest season for dishing out KO's was 1951 when he personally put to sleep twenty-one opponents. In a memorable game that year, he leveled the entire Washington Redskins backfield one by one and watched with cruel satisfaction as each victim was carted off the field.

Brown especially relished beating up the Los Angeles Rams. In 1951, he hit Rams running back Glenn Davis so hard that the ligaments in Davis' knees were torn. Then, on the last play of the game, Hardy smashed head-on into runner Dick Hoerner, sending him sprawling to the sideline. After the gun sounded, the teams went into their dressing rooms. When the Rams counted noses, they discovered that Hoerner was missing. Fifteen minutes later, they found him staggering to his feet on the sideline where Brown had tackled him. The Rams were furious and plotted to "get" Hardy the next time they played the 49ers. Each player put five dollars in a pot as a reward for the Ram who could put Brown in the hospital. But after the two teams met again, the money was returned. No one had so much as bruised Hardy.

The following year, 1952, the New York Giants tried to disable Brown after he broke the jaw of runner Joe Scott, whose teeth ended up scattered all over the field. On the next play, the whole Giants team went after Brown. He retreated to the end zone, shouting, "I can't fight them all!" Nevertheless, he managed to deck three Giants before getting pummeled.

"Brown was the meanest by a mile," declared former NFL guard and coach Chuck Drulis. "He enjoyed hurting people. He broke more noses and caved in more faces than anyone else in football. I once saw him knock out two players on the same play. It was a punt return. He got one guy with a block, got up and then laid out another. Good backs like Frank Gifford and Kyle Rote feared him. They hated to carry out fakes into the line because Hardy hit so hard."

Quarterback Y.A. Tittle recalled how Brown instilled absolute terror in running backs. "Brown was with the Redskins and I was with the Colts in 1950. Just before the game, one of our halfbacks, Rip Collins, told me, 'I don't want you to throw the ball near number 47. That's Hardy Brown and I want to keep as far away from him as I can get.' I said, 'You must be kidding.' In the third quarter, I forgot about what Collins said. I threw him a little pass and Hardy hit him. When I visited Collins in the hospital that night, I realized that he hadn't been kidding at all."

Sympathy was not in Brown's vocabulary, although he had his own unique way of being nice to his victims. During a 1953 game against the Cleveland Browns, Brown blindsided running back Billy Reynolds with such force that Reynolds ended up in the hospital for four days. The next time the Browns played the 49ers, Brown walked over to Reynolds, shook his hand, and smiled. Then in a kind, gentle voice, Hardy said, "If you come into my territory, I'll have to get you again."

MEAN JOE GREENE

Defensive Lineman · Pittsburgh Steelers · 1969–81

Mean Joe Greene was given his nickname for good reason. He *was* mean.

In his first year in the pros, Greene turned into a one-man wrecking crew and annihilated his opponents, becoming the most ferocious rookie the league had ever seen. Greene knocked out New York Giants quarterback Fran Tarkenton with a vicious late hit, punched out Minnesota Vikings guard Jim Vellone, and was thrown out of 2 games—a record a veteran meanie would have been proud of.

But Greene secured his reputation as the Master of Malice when he spit on Chicago Bears tough guy Dick Butkus—and got away with it. While the Bears were humiliating the Steelers, Butkus was blitzing at will, and Greene couldn't stand it any longer. As Butkus walked in front of the Pittsburgh bench after a play, Greene bolted toward him, swore at him, and then spit in Butkus' face. Butkus sized up the snorting-mad 6-foot, 4-inch, 270-pound lineman and turned and walked back to the security of the carnage on the field.

Mean Joe did not know the meaning of the word pity. In a game in 1974, he was outplaying Cincinnati guard Pat Matson. When Matson

started to limp off the field, Greene ran over and shouted, "Come on, I want you out here!"

During the heat of battle, Mean Joe often reached the boiling point (which for him was anything over 32 degrees). Once, after an opposing guard had hit him with a good clean block, Greene grabbed the offender by the shoulder pads and kicked him right between the legs.

It was one of several lamentable kicking performances by Mean Joe. His most brutal kick occurred in a 1975 game against the Cleveland Browns. With evil in his heart, Greene attacked offensive guard Bob McKay in a way that would have horrified even the most crazed wrestling fan. Mean Joe stomped on McKay and repeatedly kicked the prostrate lineman in the groin and legs. Finally, a gang of Browns wrestled Greene to the ground and thrashed him. For his place kicking (or kicking in place) of McKay's body, Greene was ejected from the game.

Mean Joe mellowed with age. Instead of whomping opponents with savage kicks, he socked them with sneaky punches at the snap of the ball. But his fierce cheap shots were exposed to fans during a nationally televised game in 1977. The TV audience was treated to instant replays of what decent Americans would call aggravated assault. Greene wasn't penalized by the officials because they failed to see what the cameras did. However, after reviewing the replays, the league office spanked him with a stiff fine.

As the years passed, Mean Joe matured. Instead of throwing tantrums, he hurled epithets. To the media, he offered these gentle thoughts about referees: "If they get in the way, I'll cleat 'em in the spine." "I wish a bolt of lightning would come down and strike one of their hearts out." "I'll call them the dirtiest name I can think of. I'll talk about their momma."

His rancor toward refs reached new heights during a game in Philadelphia. Greene constantly claimed he was being held, but the officials weren't calling it. Finally, before the Eagle center could snap the ball for another play, Greene swiped the pigskin and threw it into the second tier of the stands. Then he marched off the field.

ED SPRINKLE

Defensive End · Chicago Bears · 1944–55

Ed Sprinkle lived by the motto: "Do unto others before they do unto you." What he did unto others was just short of a felony.

Sprinkle's goal wasn't to knock players out of the way; it was to knock them out of the game. Busted noses and cleat-marked bodies were the legacy of the meanest defensive end in pro football.

In 1949, Sprinkle deliberately stomped on Chicago Cardinals star running back Elmer Angsman, who wound up with five cleat marks on his chest.

Fueling his reputation as a headhunter, the *Los Angeles Times* account of a 1949 Rams–Bears game reported: "The Ram attack was weakened considerably in the third quarter when fullback Dick Hoerner suffered a slight concussion after assertedly being worked over by the notorious Bear end Ed Sprinkle. Hoerner was taken to Queens of Angels hospital. . . ."

The New York Giants still haven't forgiven Sprinkle for his savagery in the 1946 championship play-off. Sprinkle did his part to ensure the 24–14 Chicago victory by incapacitating three key New York backs.

Besides separating the shoulder of George Franck, Sprinkle fractured Frank Reagan's nose and gave him a concussion. Both Giant players ended up in the hospital during the first half. Sprinkle then broke Frank Filchock's nose in the second half.

One of Sprinkle's favorite hits of all time was a knockout blow he delivered to San Francisco 49ers back Hugh McElhenny. "The San Francisco fans nearly rioted over that one," Sprinkle recalled with pride. "I launched myself at him like a rocket and damn near knocked him into the stands. It turned his helmet clean around and he told me later that when he woke up, he was looking through the holes in the back of his helmet.

"It was all part of football. I played rough. I won't deny it. I went out there to hit somebody. Hard! If the way I played hurt somebody's feelings, too bad."

Sprinkle hurt much more than feelings. If vicious forearm blows, late hits, and illegal tripping didn't slow down pass receivers, Sprinkle resorted to other devious methods, such as "chucking" and "spinning." Chucking, he explained, is when "you put out your hands as though you are pushing, but actually you are grabbing your opponent's shirt and you hold him for a one-two count—just long enough to disrupt his timing and throw him off stride." To pull off the trick of spinning, "you grab a guy's shirt as he's running by and yank. If you've got a strong grip, and your timing is right, he'll spin himself right out of the play."

During a 1948 game against the Rams, Sprinkle spun and chucked close pal and former teammate Dante Magnani, who quickly realized that past friendships meant nothing to Sprinkle. When Magnani stepped on him in retaliation, Sprinkle landed a left jab to Magnani's chin, triggering a donnybrook that ended when he and four other players were ejected.

As a pass rusher, Sprinkle tried not only to sack the quarterback, but to behead him as well. Typical of his ferociousness was the pain he inflicted in a 1951 game against the Cleveland Browns. Sprinkle rushed quarterback Otto Graham and delivered him a crushing blow to the head. The cruel move knocked Graham's helmet off and broke his nose. Graham fumbled the ball; Sprinkle scooped it up and rambled 55 yards for a touchdown.

Sometimes "Nose-breaker" Sprinkle worked himself into such a frenzy that no one was safe—not even his own teammates. In a 1948 game, Bears center Bulldog Turner got in Sprinkle's way. He ended up with a busted schnozz.

A PAIN IN THE PASS

Some passers throw bombs; other passers are bombs. They can't throw their own weight around, let alone throw a football. When they pass, it's usually from the I formation—I for incompletions and interceptions. Most of these passers couldn't hit a receiver with a shotgun. They even have trouble passing the salt at the training table. For "The Most Pitiful Passes Ever Thrown," The Football Hall of SHAME inducts the following:

GARO YEPREMIAN

Placekicker • Miami Dolphins • Jan. 14, 1973

Garo Yepremian attempted the most foolhardy pass ever seen in a Super Bowl game—and it nearly cost his team a perfect season.

With the Miami Dolphins leading the Washington Redskins 14–0 in the final 2 minutes of Super Bowl VII, Yepremian attempted a 42-yard field goal to ice the game. But his kick was blocked.

Rather than prudently fall on the loose ball, Yepremian picked it up, which wasn't smart. In an even dumber move, the pint-sized Cypriot tried to *pass* the ball. It hung on his fingertips for half a second, then slipped out of his hand. Washington safety Mike Bass plucked the ball out of the air and raced 49 yards for a lucky touchdown.

Yepremian's debut as a Super Bowl passer sent shock waves through Miami partisans and created fears of total disaster. Fortunately for the team—and for the boneheaded kicker-turned-passer—the Dolphins held on for a 14–7 triumph to cap a flawless season.

"I thought I was doing something good, something to help the team," said Yepremian after the game. "Instead it was almost a tragedy."

The next day on the plane home, Dolphin coach Don Shula summoned Yepremian. The little kicker was hesitant until he noticed Shula was all smiles. "You know that pass you threw yesterday?" asked Shula, whose tone of voice didn't match his smile. "If you ever try it again, I'll kill you."

JIM HARDY

Quarterback • Chicago Cardinals • Sept. 24, 1950

Jim Hardy led the Philadelphia Eagles to a 45–7 rout over the Chicago Cardinals by completing eight passes to the Eagles and setting up five of their six touchdowns. The only problem was that Hardy played for the Cardinals at the time.

Throwing to his defenders almost as often as he did to his receivers, Hardy suffered the worst day ever for an NFL quarterback. He tossed a league record 8 interceptions and fumbled 3 times.

Hardy should have stayed in bed. On the way to the game, he smashed up his car. Considering how the rest of the afternoon went, the car crash was the day's bright spot. Hardy arrived at the stadium just in time for the kickoff and entered the game without so much as a single warmup toss.

On his first series, Hardy tried to pass to end Bob Shaw, but was hit just as he threw. The ball landed right in the arms of Eagle defensive back Joe Sutton, who was on the Philadelphia 40-yard line. Ten plays later, the Eagles scored a touchdown. They soon converted a Hardy fumble into a field goal for a 10–0 lead.

On the first play of the second quarter, Hardy threw another errant pass, this time to Eagle defensive back Russ Craft, who ran the ball back 20 yards to the Chicago 14-yard line. It took Philadelphia only 3 plays to hike the score to 17–0.

Just 2 minutes later, Hardy gifted the ball to the Eagles again. Philadelphia tackle Jay MacDowell graciously accepted Hardy's fumbled ball on the Cardinal 15-yard line. After such a helpful present, the Eagles scored in 3 plays for a 24–0 lead. Late in the quarter, Hardy threw his third interception. By halftime, Hardy had boosted the Eagles' margin to 31–0.

"I really felt low at halftime," Hardy recalled. "I can still remember sitting on a bench in the dressing room with my head in my hands thinking that nothing could be worse than 3 interceptions in one half. Little did I know I was to have 5 more."

Hardy's generosity knew no limits. He opened the second half by losing a fumble on his own 26-yard line. One play later, the Eagles led 38–0. On the very next play after the kickoff, Hardy threw his fourth interception, which was run back 74 yards for another TD. The score was now 45–0.

Midway through the third quarter, it finally dawned on Chicago coach Curly Lambeau that maybe this just wasn't Hardy's day. Lambeau benched him in favor of Frank Tripucka. Hardy's assault on the interception record was in serious jeopardy until fate lent a hand; after only 3 plays, Tripucka was carried off the field with a knee injury. So Hardy was sent back in to the game and allowed his date with destiny.

Hardy passed as if he were color bind. His favorite receivers wore Eagle green rather than Cardinal red as Russ Craft picked off 4 Hardy tosses and Joe Sutton snared 3.

Some of the discredit for Hardy's ignoble achievement must go to an offensive line so weak it couldn't block out the sun with an umbrella. On almost every pass attempt, Hardy was scrambling for his life and throwing the ball up for grabs in desperation. He attempted 39 passes, completing 12 to his own teammates and 8 to the Eagles.

"I felt so bad that day," said Hardy, "that after the game I was wishing I was a mole so I could burrow my way out of the place under the grass."

SAMMY BAUGH

Quarterback • Washington Redskins • Dec. 16, 1945

Sammy Baugh waited until the 1945 championship game to throw the most mortifying pass of his stellar pro career. Worse yet, Slingin' Sammy's unforgettable toss lost the title game for his Washington Redskins.

Early in the first quarter in a scoreless battle with the Cleveland Rams, the Redskins were backed up near their own goal. Trying to dig out of the hole, Baugh called for a pass. End Wayne Millner scampered past a startled and beaten Cleveland secondary. Meanwhile, Baugh faded back into the end zone, saw his man wide open, and threw with all his might.

It would have been a stupendous play had the ball made it out of the end zone. To Baugh's horror, the ball slipped off his fingers, smacked right into the goal post, and fluttered to the ground in the end zone for an automatic safety. Back then, the rule stated: "When a forward pass from behind the goal line strikes the goal posts or the crossbar . . . it is a safety if the pass strikes the ground in the end zone."

The 2 points awarded to Cleveland decided the outcome of the NFL championship game. The safety enabled the Rams to squeak by the Redskins 15–14.

After the game, Washington owner George Marshall received a detailed explanation of the safety rule from the referees. Then he thundered, "Well, I'm sure as hell going to change that rule at our next league meeting." And he sure as hell did. The following year, the rule stated that such a pass would be called incomplete. Unfortunately, they didn't pass the rule soon enough for poor Sammy.

GEORGE "KID" WOODRUFF

Quarterback • Georgia Bulldogs • Nov. 5, 1910

Georgia's Kid Woodruff threw college football's sneakiest pass.

It happened during a fiercely fought game played in a dense fog on a Tennessee mountaintop field where the Sewanee Tigers were beating the Georgia Bulldogs 15–6 late in the fourth quarter. For Georgia, this was a desperate situation requiring desperate measures.

The Bulldogs had the ball on the Sewanee 30-yard line when Woodruff took the snap and faded back to pass into the mist. Hiding the ball in one hand, he quickly whipped off his leather headgear and flung it as hard as he could into the fog down the left sideline toward a sprinting Bulldog receiver. Naturally, the Tiger secondary reacted to the "pass" and gave chase.

Assured that he had tricked them, Woodruff passed the real pigskin to halfback Bob McWhorter, who scampered down the right sideline for a touchdown.

POOP TALKS

Pep talks are designed by coaches to inspire their teams and to infuse their players with the desire to go beyond their limits. Too often, however, the coaches are the ones who go beyond the limits—of taste, propriety, and zeal. There should be a penalty for illegal use of the tongue. For "The Most Deplorable Pep Talks Ever Delivered," The Football Hall of SHAME inducts the following:

DAN DEVINE

Coach ▪ Missouri Tigers ▪ Nov. 18, 1967

No matter how well plays are devised, they don't always work out the way the coach had planned. Dan Devine found the same was true with pep talks.

To rev up his Tigers for a game against Nebraska, Devine decided to make his team sick of the Cornhuskers' fight song.

In 1966, Nebraska whipped Missouri 35–0, and the band had played "There Is No Place Like Nebraska" every time the Huskers scored. The Tigers had gotten a real earful of the song because the band sat right behind their bench.

Devine hated the song so much that he figured hearing it would rile up his own team and spur them on to victory in 1967. On the Monday prior to the game, he ordered the team manager to play only one record in the Missouri locker room throughout the week—the Nebraska fight song. That's all the Tigers heard every day as they changed, showered, and dressed.

By game day, Devine had primed his players for a special pep talk that was guaranteed to motivate them. "I never want to hear that song again!" he thundered at the Tigers. Then he grabbed the offending record and, with all his might, flung it to the cement floor in the locker room.

Devine had expected the disk to break into a hundred pieces, under-scoring his words and leaving a lasting visual impact with the players before they charged out onto the field. But things didn't go according to plan. To his everlasting chagrin, the record didn't break. Instead, it bounced straight up and hit the ceiling.

That was Devine's first clue that he was in danger of both bungling his message and losing his composure. He picked up the record and slammed it to the floor a second time. But, once again, it survived. Clenching his teeth, Devine tried to snap the record in two with his bare hands. The record bent, but it didn't break. His face red with anger and frustration, Devine hurled the record against the wall. It bounced back like a tennis ball.

"I don't know when I've ever been so embarrassed and humiliated," Devine recalled. "Finally, I just went over to a window, opened it, and threw the record out. Then I got out of there as fast as I could."

Despite their coach's deplorable performance, the Tigers won 10–7.

KNUTE ROCKNE

Coach ▪ Notre Dame Fighting Irish ▪ Oct. 28, 1922

Knute Rockne would do anything to psych up his team before a big game—even lie through his teeth.

For a game against Georgia Tech in Atlanta, where the Yellow Jackets had been undefeated for several years, Rockne felt his underdog team needed an inspirational lift.

He strode into the locker room and showed the players several telegrams of encouragement from prominent alumni. Then he told his team, "I have one wire here, boys, that probably doesn't mean much to you, but it does to me." He took a deep breath and his voice began to crack. "It's from my poor sick little boy Billy, who is critically ill in the hospital."

Rockne's throat tightened, his lips trembled, and his eyes watered as he read Billy's poignant wire: "I want Daddy's team to win."

Touched by this tear-jerking request from the coach's ailing son, the Irish roared out of the locker room and ripped apart Georgia Tech 13–3.

When the victorious team arrived back in South Bend, Indiana, an ecstatic crowd of 20,000 fans greeted the Irish at the train station. And who was skipping about in front of all the well-wishers? None other than "sick" little Billy Rockne, in picture-perfect health.

Billy hadn't been ill at all. Rockne had sent the bogus telegram himself.

That wasn't the only time Rockne resorted to a cock-and-bull story. Before the November 16, 1929 game against the University of Southern California, Rockne told alumnus Joe Byrne, "We're going to lose today. The team has been lethargic all week. The only way to win is if I can think of something that would give the boys an emotional lift."

In the locker room, Rockne told his team, "Boys, I'm getting this pressure from the alumni. My wife Bonnie can't take it any longer, and my children are being ridiculed at school. I am resigning. Please let me go out a winner. So go out there and win, WIN!"

Notre Dame beat USC 13–12. Afterward, Byrne asked Rockne, "What are you going to tell the boys when you see them at practice next Monday?"

"What do you mean, what will I tell them? I *am* resigning—unless I get a letter of apology from the alumni."

Rockne had told such a good fib that he had even convinced himself it was true!

GRANT TEAFF

Coach • Baylor Bears • Nov. 25, 1978

In what may be the most disgusting climax to a pre-game pep talk ever given, Grant Teaff made his Baylor Bears watch him eat a worm.

What this had to do with football was anybody's guess. Nevertheless, the Bears did charge out of the locker room with such ferocity that they broke the hinges off the door. That was no surprise. They all wanted to throw up.

Teaff bit off more than he could chew at the end of a week of preparation for a game against the highly favored Texas Longhorns. Because Baylor was going to limp into the contest with an awful 2–8 record and several key players injured, Teaff decided that his team needed to stay loose.

So, during a team meeting, Teaff told the players a funny story about two Eskimos fishing through the ice. One was catching fish and the other wasn't. The unsuccessful angler asked his partner what his secret was. The successful fisherman opened his mouth, pulled out a slimy worm, and replied, "You've got to keep the worms warm."

The tale gave Teaff a nauseating idea. On the day of the game, he bought a box of worms, cleaned one of them, and put it in his pocket. Moments before game time, he told his players, "The game is yours, but there's one thing I'll do for you. I'll keep the worms warm." Then he took the worm out, dropped it in his mouth, and ate it.

Strangely, the Bears were inspired by Teaff's revolting pep talk, and they destroyed mighty Texas 38–14.

Later, one of the players approached the coach and said, "I noticed you turned a bright shade of purple after eating the worm. How did it taste?" Replied Teaff, "About like you'd expect a damn worm to taste."

AP/WIDE WORLD PHOTOS

CURLY LAMBEAU

Coach • Green Bay Packers • Dec. 11, 1938

As the second quarter ended in the championship game between the Green Bay Packers and the New York Giants, Curly Lambeau was contemplating what to tell his players.

He knew this would be one of the most important chalk talks of his coaching career. With the Packers losing 16–14, the players would look to him for a revised game plan. Coming up with the right strategy, adjustments, and motivating words could turn the halftime deficit into a victory.

Incredibly, through his numskullery, Lambeau never did give that crucial talk. He was so lost in thought on his way to the locker room that he ended up lost in the stadium.

Lingering behind his players, Lambeau somehow made a wrong turn under the Polo Grounds. He opened the door to what he thought was the clubhouse and wound up out on the street. Before he realized his error, the door slammed shut behind him and he was locked out.

The coach frantically pounded on the door to no avail, then raced to the nearest gate. But the guard refused to let him in. "If you're the coach, what are you doing out here on the sidewalk?" the guard asked snidely.

Swearing a blue streak, Lambeau hustled off to another gate. But no amount of pleading, cajoling, or threatening could get him past the next guard, who shoved him away with the sarcastic refrain, "Yeah, sure, and I'm the King of England."

Meanwhile, back in the locker room, the Packers were wondering what had happened to their coach. Back then, teams didn't have the

cadre of assistants that today's clubs have. As the halftime minutes elapsed, the perplexed players couldn't agree on a revised game plan.

Unbeknownst to them, their angry, red-faced coach had now charged into the main gate, only to be stopped once again. Spewing the vilest language of his life at the top of his lungs, Lambeau attracted a big crowd, including some reporters.

The scribes immediately recognized Lambeau and convinced the guards that he was indeed the Green Bay coach. By the time he reached the locker room, the second half was about to begin. Without Lambeau's crucial halftime instructions, the Packers faltered in the last 2 quarters and lost 23–17.

WALLY BUTTS

Coach · Georgia Bulldogs · Oct. 26, 1946

Wally Butts was nicknamed "Weeping Wally" because he always told sob stories about his team's poor chances of winning—even during 1946, when the Bulldogs went undefeated. Only once, in an ill-advised halftime pep talk that year, did he have good reason to cry.

Weeping Wally was in rare form before his top-rated team took the field against hapless Furman University in Greenville, South Carolina. He had already lamented to the press that his team was decimated by injuries and was in no condition to be playing Furman. One local reporter actually believed him and predicted an upset.

As usual, Butts was just blowing smoke. But he didn't want anyone to know that, especially his own players. Even though the Bulldogs were leading 28–7 at the half and had totally dominated the game, Butts read them the riot act in the locker room. "That's the sorriest exhibition of football I've ever seen," he railed. "Y'all ought to be behind 28–7 instead of ahead. It's just terrible."

Suddenly, Butts ran toward a fired-up, pot-bellied stove in the middle of the dressing room and kicked it. The pipe connecting the stove to the ceiling broke loose and, to Butts's complete mortification, a cloud of soot dusted him in black. To make matters worse, he hurt his foot so badly he thought he had broken it.

"He's holding his foot and cussing us out and we're having to bite our lips to keep from laughing," recalled Porter Payne, a guard on the team. "Then he got so tickled at how absurd the scene was that he was about to burst out laughing, so he bit his tongue and limped out of the room."

Oh, by the way, Georgia won 70–7.

DEFENSELESS DEFENSES

Some defenses are so weak they need security guards to protect them. Even the Munchkins could knock them on their butts. By year's end, they usually give up enough ground to form a new continent. That's because their nickel defense isn't worth five cents, and their pass rush is more like a pass stroll. For "The Weakest Defensive Performances," The Football Hall of SHAME inducts the following:

CUMBERLAND COLLEGE

Oct. 7, 1916

No team ever suffered a more devastating, more overwhelming defeat than Cumberland College. The team was crushed 222–0.

Blame the worst shellacking in collegiate history on poor field position—Cumberland had to play on the same field with the Georgia Tech Yellow Jackets.

Tackling dummies would have put up a better defense. The losers were so powerless that the Yellow Jackets scored on every single possession. Never before or since has a college team given up so many points (222), touchdowns (32), and yards (968) in one game. Thirteen TDs came on returns of interceptions, fumbles, punts, and kickoffs. Tech ran the ball only 29 times, and hit pay dirt on 19 of those carries. The Yellow Jackets netted 528 yards on the ground so there was no need to pass. An additional 220 yards came on punt returns and another 220 yards on kickoff returns.

It was a mismatch even before the players donned their uniforms in Atlanta. Cumberland, a little school in Lebanon, Tennessee, had an informal pickup team coached by a law student, Butch McQueen. The bigger college boasted a powerful football program headed by the

brilliant coach John Heisman (for whom the famous football trophy is named). Cumberland's team was made up of serious students who pored over textbooks; Tech's squad consisted of athletes who studied mostly play books. Cumberland rounded up 16 students who were foolish enough to play Tech. One of them, who had virtually no football experience, joined the team because he wanted to take his first Pullman ride. The Yellow Jackets were coming off an unbeaten season the previous year and viewed the game as nothing more than an easy tune-up on the new schedule.

Realizing that Napoleon stood a better chance of success at Waterloo than Cumberland did at Tech's Grant Field, the officials at the Tennessee school wanted to call the game off. But because of an earlier agreement between the two schools, the tiny college had to field a team or forfeit $3,000 in good-faith money. The school decided to risk life and limb rather than lose the three grand. When the squad assembled for the trip to Atlanta, three players missed the train. They were either very smart or very lucky.

Although the Cumberland players didn't bother to practice, they genuinely believed they could play a respectable game. They didn't expect to beat Tech. But they didn't expect to become victims of the most horrendous rout in Atlanta since General Sherman sacked the city in 1864.

The turning point of the game came during the flip of the coin. Tech won the toss and chose to kick off. The play resulted in Cumberland's "first down"—the quarterback was knocked unconscious and carted off the field. He was the fortunate one. He didn't have to experience the 2½ hours of pain and suffering inflicted on his teammates.

On the first play from scrimmage, Cumberland running back Morris Gouger plowed into the Tech line for a 3-yard gain. It was the highlight of the half for Cumberland. Unable to move the ball any further, Cumberland punted, and Tech's Everett Strupper returned the ball to the Cumberland 20-yard line. On the very next play he scored a TD, one of 8 he tallied on that unbelievable day.

On the ensuing kickoff, Cumberland fumbled the ball. Tech scooped it up and hauled it in for a second touchdown. The drubbing had begun.

Trailing 28–0 midway through the first quarter, Cumberland came up with a new strategy. Since waving a white flag only works on the battlefield, they tried the next best thing—they surrendered the football. Believing they would be better off with the ball in Tech's territory, Cumberland began kicking off rather than receiving after every Tech score. But the Yellow Jackets returned the first such kickoff 70 yards and scored 2 plays later. The next kickoff was returned only 40 yards, but they again hit pay dirt on the first play from scrimmage. Tech soared to a 63–0 lead—at the end of the *first quarter*. By halftime, Tech's point total had doubled.

Showing the mercy of the Marquis de Sade, Heisman told his troops between halves, "Men, we're in front, but you never know what those Cumberland players have up their sleeves. So in the second half, go out and hit 'em clean and hit 'em hard. Don't let up."

Heisman deliberately wanted to run up the score to prove a point. Sportswriters back then had a tendency to rate teams solely on how many points they scored. Heisman thought this was a poor way to judge the worth of a team, so he chose the Cumberland game to show how easy—and meaningless—it was to beat up a weak team.

Try as they might, the Yellow Jackets could tally only 96 points in the second half. The Tech backs were near exhaustion from running up and down the field, so Heisman let the tackles carry the ball. Thirteen players managed to score in the blowout.

Meanwhile, Cumberland had the offensive punch of a glassy-eyed boxer. The team's biggest play of the day was a 10-yard pass. But it didn't help much. It was third-and-28. Unable to make a single first down, Cumberland rushed for minus 45 yards, completed 2 of 11 passes for a total of 14 yards, threw 4 interceptions, and fumbled 9 times.

One of those fumbles was a botched snap from center. After his bungle, quarterback Leon McDonald pointed to the bounding ball and shouted to backfield mate Morris Gouger, "Pick it up! Pick it up!" But Gouger, battered and weary from all the vicious tackling, saw the big Tech linemen crashing in and yelled back to McDonald, "Pick it up yourself. It's *your* fumble."

Early in the fourth quarter, Heisman spotted an exhausted Cumberland player hiding under a blanket on the Tech bench. "Son," said the coach gently, "you're on the wrong bench."

"Oh no I'm not," replied the fatigued player. "This is the Georgia Tech side, isn't it?"

"Yes."

"Well, then, this is the only place I'm safe. If I go back to my bench, I'm liable to get sent back in the game again!"

HOUSTON COUGARS

Nov. 23, 1968

After getting slaughtered 100–6 by the Houston Cougars, the Tulsa Golden Hurricane certainly qualified for induction into The Football Hall of SHAME. After all, Tulsa had set a modern major college record by giving up 100 points.

However, due to mitigating circumstances, Houston, not Tulsa, deserves the boos.

Although the city of Houston has gained a reputation in the field of medicine for saving hearts, the Houston Cougars earned a stigma on the football field for being *heartless*. Not content with the ruthless 51–6 third-quarter beating it was inflicting on an injury-riddled, flu-stricken, blatantly outclassed team, Houston unveiled its malevolence by rolling up a record 49 fourth-quarter points.

The seed for the lopsided victory was planted a year earlier after the Hurricane upset the visiting Cougars 22–13 in the final game of 1967. The defeat cost Houston what would have been its first ever Top Ten finish. Cougar coach Bill Yeoman left the field in a huff, refusing to shake the hand of Tulsa coach Glenn Dobbs. "Wait until we get you back in our place next year!" Yeoman declared.

The next year, the Hurricane players knew they didn't stand a ghost of a chance of winning. Houston, one of the nation's hottest teams, was headed for an NCAA record for total offense. Tulsa, on the other hand, belonged in a hospital ward. Fifteen starters and a host of reserves were suffering from the flu. Four other first-stringers were out with injuries. The squad was so decimated there was talk of their offering to forfeit. But the Hurricane players were too proud. They wanted to give it their all—which, unfortunately, wasn't very much.

Nevertheless, Tulsa trailed only 24–6 early in the third quarter. But soon fever and fatigue began to take its toll, and the defense began to wilt. Yeoman, the merciless Cougar coach, wanted to run up the score and pad his team's offensive statistics, so he kept in his first string. Not until he had a 45-point lead going into the final quarter did he send in his fresh and eager second unit to carve up the weak and demoralized Hurricane defense.

Houston relentlessly made 7 fourth-period touchdowns on a 34-yard interception return, a 58-yard punt return, runs of 11 and 3 yards, and passes of 18, 26, and 27 yards. It was a tribute to the Astrodome scoreboard that it didn't blow a fuse.

The Cougars didn't let up. With each touchdown, the 34,098 blood-thirsty homecoming fans demanded more. They kept screaming for 100 points and didn't shut up until their team obliged them.

Late in the game, Larry Gatlin (yes, *the* Larry Gatlin of country music fame), a reserve who didn't play enough to earn a varsity letter, caught a 27-yard touchdown pass for his only collegiate TD. That made the score 93–6 with a little more than 4 minutes left to play.

All Tulsa had to do was control the ball to avoid the ultimate indignity. Alas, the Hurricane offense was just as pitiful as its defense and decided to punt. Luckily, however, there were only 30 seconds remaining. What more misery could happen in so short a time? Here's what: Houston's Mike Simpson caught the punt on his 42-yard line and raced virtually untouched all the way to the end zone, boosting the Cougars' point total to 99.

The chant from the crowd of "One hundred! One hundred!" was deafening as placekicker Terry Leiweke, who complained he was getting leg cramps from kicking so much, stepped onto the field to try for his 13th extra point. The pressure was on, but he responded by booting the ball through the uprights for Houston's 100th point. Leiweke was mobbed by his point-hungry teammates and cheered by the deliriously happy fans.

When the carnage was over, the Cougars had ravaged the sickly Hurricane for 37 first downs and 762 yards in total offense. They had scored 76 points in the second half for yet another modern NCAA record.

When questioned by reporters after the game, Yeoman denied he had run up the score. Amazingly, he was able to say this with a straight face. His counterpart, Dobbs, refused to shake his hand after the game, and said very little to the press.

"No team deserves this kind of treatment," said Tulsa player David Moss years later. "To get beat and get your nose rubbed in it is the most devastating thing for an athlete.

"It was humiliating. I wanted to just hide under my bed and not come out for a year."

WASHINGTON REDSKINS

Dec. 8, 1940

The Washington Redskins suffered the most lopsided rout in the annals of pro football. The Chicago Bears clobbered them 73–0.

They were beaten even before they stepped foot on the field. And for that, they can blame their owner, George Preston Marshall.

Three weeks before the debacle, the Redskins knocked off the Bears 7–3 after a questionable last-second call by an official robbed Chicago of the winning touchdown. A chortling George Marshall added insult to injury when he told the press, "The Bears are quitters. They're not a second-half team, just a bunch of crybabies. They fold up when the going gets tough." Less than a month later, Marshall choked on his own words.

In the Bears' locker room at Washington's Griffith Stadium moments before the NFL championship game against those same Redskins, Chicago coach George Halas handed his players clippings of Marshall's remarks. "Gentlemen," said Halas, "this is what George Preston Marshall thinks of you. I think you're a great football team. Go out on the field and prove it!"

They did.

Two and a half hours later, the Bears had racked up an astounding 73 points—to this day the most ever scored in any NFL game—while the Redskins had failed to score.

The fired-up Chicago team struck right away. The game was only 55 seconds old when fullback Bill Osmanski skirted around left end and raced 68 yards for a touchdown. The Bears tallied 21 points in the first 13 minutes and led 28–0 at the half. Contrary to Marshall's opinion of them, the Bears didn't quit at halftime. In the final 30 minutes, they scored 45 more points.

The Bears riddled the Redskins with a relentless ground game and kept them at bay with an overwhelming defense. Halas used all 33 eligible men on his squad and 15 of them scored. The only question that remained in the second half was whether Chicago would score more points when they were on offense or when they were on defense. The Bears piled up 501 yards of total offense and picked off 8 Redskin passes, returning 3 for touchdowns.

Washington couldn't do anything right—and it rubbed off on the public address announcer. With the score 60–0, he displayed just as poor judgment and timing as the losing home team when he told the crowd, "Your attention is directed to a very important announcement regarding the sale of seats for the 1941 Redskin season." What few Washington fans were left in the stadium suddenly broke their silence with a thunderous round of boos and then lapsed back into a state of depression.

After the Bears scored their tenth TD, one of the officials asked Halas if he would mind *not* trying to kick for the extra point. So many balls had been booted into the stands and carried away by fans that the officials were down to their last football. Halas, feeling magnanimous with the 66-point lead, instructed his team to pass for the last 2 extra-point attempts (one of which they made).

When the final gun sounded, one reporter in the press box announced, in jest, "Marshall just shot himself!" Later, in the locker room, Marshall didn't have much to say about the unprecedented pounding other than, "We needed a 50-man line against their power."

Arthur Daley of *The New York Times* wrote: "So one-sided was the match that press box critics could not single out any of the Redskin players for praise. There was no Redskin hero outside of coach Ray Flaherty, who had to sit on the bench and absorb it all, too much a beating for so fine a gentleman and coach. At the end, the Redskin band played 'Should Auld Acquaintance Be Forgot,' If said acquaintance is the Chicago Bears, it should be forgot immediately."

In the somber loser's locker room, reporters told Washington quarterback Sammy Baugh they felt the turning point of the game came early in the first quarter when receiver Charley Malon dropped a sure touchdown pass that would have tied the game.

"If Malon had caught that pass," a sportswriter asked Baugh, "wouldn't it have been an entirely different game?"

"Yeh," said Baugh. "The score would have been 73–7."

OKLAHOMA STATE

Nov. 5, 1904

Oklahoma State was the only football team to be annihilated not only on the field but in the water as well.

In the first game ever between the Oklahoma Sooners and Oklahoma State (then known as the Oklahoma A & M Aggies), the teams met halfway between their schools in the town of South Guthrie. They played on a field bordered by the icy red waters of Cottonwood Creek on a cold, blustery, cloudy day.

The underdog Aggies were small, inexperienced, and coached by a music teacher. Hundreds of spectators, wrapped in overcoats, scarfs, and gloves, shivered along the sidelines as they waited for the kickoff to signal the beginning of an anticipated rout. The Aggies, however, still thought they could win.

On the fourth play of the game, any hopes for an upset were sunk—literally. State's B.O. Callahan stood in his own end zone and punted the ball up into a brisk wind. The ball was blown straight into the surging, murky waters of Cottonwood Creek, where it bobbed and floated like a cork as the swift current swept it downstream past the Aggies' goal line. In those days, a loose ball became the property of the team that recovered it, no matter how far it went beyond the field boundaries. If a Sooner recovered the ball, it would be a touchdown.

State's Robert Baird was trying to fish the ball out of the creek with a stick when Sooner tackle Becker Matthews ran up behind him and knocked him into the water. Then Matthews, realizing that Baird was close to snatching the ball, splashed into the freezing water after him. Battling in midstream, where the water was over their heads, they fought for the wet, slippery pigskin, but it kept squirting through their fingers. Matthews beat Baird back by dunking him. Baird, who couldn't swim, managed to thrash his way back to shore and crawl out of the water.

By now, players from both teams had leaped into the creek, fully clad in heavy football gear. But the Sooners overpowered the weaker Aggies. Oklahoma's Ed Cook, a strong swimmer, finally reached the ball and carried it back to the bank behind the Aggie goal line for the oddest touchdown in collegiate history.

While the crowd roared with laughter, the waterlogged players scrambled out of the creek and faced the bone-chilling wind. Their teeth chattering, the players finished the rest of the first half in their soaking-wet duds. Between halves, the starters ordered their substitutes to hand over their dry uniforms.

As badly as they performed in the water, the Aggies were even worse on land. Oklahoma roared through the weak State defense at will for a 75–0 thrashing. Every Sooner starter scored a touchdown—even the center, Roy Waggoner. He hit pay dirt when he snapped the ball, stepped back, took a lateral from the quarterback, and thundered around end for the touchdown.

Wet or dry, the Aggies were no match for the Sooners.

FLORIDA GATORS

Nov. 27, 1971

In the most shameful defensive play ever witnessed on a college gridiron, the Florida Gators literally laid down on the job.

Wanting the ball back so their quarterback could have a last-minute crack at a national record, the Gators deliberately allowed the other team to score. The least Florida could have done was pretend to tackle the runner. Instead of performing like football players, the boys from Gainesville overacted with the subtlety of a burlesque show.

There was absolutely no defense for the way the Gators staged their infamous "Florida Flop."

The Gators (3–7) were slaughtering the 4–5 Miami Hurricanes 45–8. With 2 minutes left in the game, Miami had a first down on Florida's 24-yard line.

Meanwhile, Gator senior quarterback John Reaves stood helplessly on the sideline, just 13 yards shy of Jim Plunkett's collegiate career record for passing yardage. It didn't look like Reaves would get a final shot at the coveted mark. Florida fans, informed of the situation on their portable radios, began chanting, "Let 'em score, let 'em score!"

Defensive back and co-captain Harvin Clark called time and asked his coach, Doug Dickey, "Why don't we let 'em go ahead and score?" Dickey refused.

(Ironically, Clark had cost Reaves an excellent opportunity to break the record earlier in the fourth quarter when he returned a punt 82 yards for a touchdown.)

Keeping the ball on the ground, the Hurricanes chewed up yardage and time as they pushed down to the 7-yard line. Once again, Clark called time out. He trotted to the sidelines and pleaded with Dickey, "The score isn't going to matter. Let 'em punch it in."

Dickey pondered the request for about 10 seconds and then said, "Okay, let 'em have it."

Grinning from ear to ear, Clark scampered back to the huddle and told his teammates, "We're going to let 'em score. When they hike the ball, everybody just fall on the ground."

After the ball was snapped, the Gators made absolutely no effort to play defense. They simply flopped to the ground as if they had been mowed down by a machine gun. Although disgusted by the lay-down, Miami quarterback John Hornibrook ran in for the "gimmee" touchdown.

(When Florida got the ball back, Reaves had 1:06 to break the record. On second down, he rolled out and completed a 15-yard pass to Carlos Alvarez. Reaves was now the leading college passer of all time. For the Miami game, he completed 33 of 50 passes for 348 yards. His career total of 7,549 yards exceeded Plunkett's mark by 5 yards.)

Miami coach Fran Curci was raging mad over the Florida Flop. "It was the worst thing I have ever seen in football," he charged. "I used to admire Doug Dickey as a coach—his record speaks for itself. But tonight I lost all respect for him as a coach and as a man. What he did shows absolutely no class."

Dickey claimed he did not give his Gators instructions to fall down like that. "We've never coached them on what to do to let another team score," he said. Dickey should have given them acting lessons.

THE REAR END OF THE FRONT OFFICE

Football team owners and banana-republic dictators are much alike. They can do what they want because nobody's going to stop them. The only difference between the two is that owners last longer. There are no armed revolts in football. With no one to answer to, owners have hatched outrageous schemes out of greed, ignorance, or nastiness. For "The Most Odious Actions by Owners," The Football Hall of SHAME inducts the following:

WALTER LINGO

Owner ▪ Oorang Indians ▪ 1922–23

Walter Lingo made a mockery of the NFL. Lingo, owner and operator of the world-renowned Oorang dog kennels in LaRue, Ohio, fielded a pro football team solely to promote his new breed, Oorang Airedales.

Lingo was not a big football fan, but he was a shrewd businessman. He figured that football was the best way to attract thousands of potential customers. So he bought an NFL franchise for $100 and hired Jim Thorpe to round up a team of Indians.

Lingo shunned home games. He forced his team to play almost exclusively on the road, where they could draw big crowds in major cities and best advertise his dogs in special exhibitions before the games and at halftimes. He didn't care how badly the team played. All that really mattered to him was how good Thorpe and company made his dogs look.

In order to make the team, Thorpe's Indians needed skills that had nothing to do with running, blocking, passing, or tackling. Their talents included Indian dancing, tomahawk tossing, knife throwing, and lariat twirling, all of which they displayed for the crowd's delight.

Lingo's Airedales joined the Indians in bizarre pre-game exhibitions. After Indian marksmen dazzled the crowd with fancy shooting, the Airedales retrieved the targets. The dogs also trailed and treed a live bear. Then one of the players, 195-pound Nikolas Lassa (called "Long Time Sleep" because he was so hard to wake up in the morning) wrestled the bear.

At halftime, the Indians, portraying U.S. and German soldiers engaged in armed confrontation, staged a World War I battle scene so that the Oorang Airedale "Red Cross" could provide first aid. After such a ridiculous spectacle, Lingo's players could hardly be blamed for not taking their football seriously.

As a result of Lingo's unabashed ballyhooing, his team's performance on the field was a doggone shame. In the two years they played, the Oorang Indians managed only 4 NFL victories. In nearly half their games, they failed to score a single touchdown, often losing by such horrendous scores as 62–0, 57–0, and 41–0.

Off the field, Lingo let his team behave like a pack of wild mongrels. Once, in a Chicago bar, when the bartender wanted to close up his tavern, the Indians tossed him into a telephone booth, turned it upside down, and drank until dawn. That afternoon they went out and got slaughtered by the Chicago Bears.

Whenever there was a carnival in town, the team put up their big man, Nikolas Lassa, against the carney strongman for a boxing match. Used to wrestling a bear in pre-game exhibitions, Lassa had little trouble going the required distance with a mere human. He almost always won the $20 that allowed the whole team to party all night.

Luckily for football, both the Indians and the Airedales finally went to the dogs; Lingo disbanded the team when its novelty wore off. Even with Jim Thorpe and a passel of adorable animals, Lingo's circus was one of the earliest examples of idiocy to prove that no matter how exciting the halftime entertainment (or how self-serving), nothing is more appealing to fans than a good, old-fashioned football game.

GEORGE MARSHALL

Owner • Washington Redskins • 1946

If George Marshall had run the Selective Service during World War II, the United States would have lost the war. He drafted men solely on a

whim. At least the Selective Service established some standards for picking personnel.

Marshall foolishly let the Redskins' scouting system crumble from neglect and lack of money. Instead of listening to the advice of seasoned professionals, the lunkhead scanned the sports pages and sports magazines to find his draft choices and let the pro scouts be damned. Marshall was so witless that he threw away the Redskins' No. 1 draft pick for two consecutive years—on the same player. It was a dubious feat unmatched in the annals of the NFL.

In 1945, the thick-headed owner became enamored of UCLA All-America Cal Rossi, and made him the team's top draft choice. Much to Marshall's chagrin, he later discovered what all the other NFL teams already knew—Rossi had another year of college eligibility left.

So the chief Redskin waited until 1946, when he again chose Rossi as his No. 1 pick. Unfortunately, Marshall soon learned another interesting fact about Rossi—one that the owner's better-informed colleagues already knew. Rossi wasn't even interested in playing professional football.

Marshall's draft selection was so brainless that of the thirty collegiate players he chose in 1946, he managed to sign only one.

HARRY WISMER

Owner · New York Titans · 1962

Harry Wismer's New York Titans of the AFL stand unchallenged as the worst-managed, most unprofessional team in pro football history.

Their motto was: "Don't cash your paycheck with anybody you like."

Wismer's checks bounced like fumbled footballs. To the Titans, "down-and-out" meant more than just a pass play. They were thrown for more losses off the field than on it.

The first hint of serious money problems emerged when the players didn't get paid for their final exhibition game of the preseason. From then on, the financial worries piled up like a vicious gang tackle.

Throughout the week before the Titans' second regular season game in San Diego, Wismer tried to save money by having his team practice on a high school field 45 minutes from their hotel. The field consisted of clay baked so solid that it would have been a perfect training ground for the Afrika Korps. On the final day of practice, the team bus didn't show up to take the players back to the hotel because the bus company hadn't been paid. Several veterans commandeered the cars of some high school girls. The remaining two dozen Titans, dragging their pads, helmets, and shoes behind them, trudged to the nearest main road and hitched rides.

After the fifth game, the Titans went on strike. According to league rules, paychecks had to be delivered within 24 hours after a game. The team's checks were eight *days* overdue. The players gave Wismer an ultimatum: "No pay, no play." Wismer responded by threatening to put the whole team on waivers and forbade his coaches to coach. The Titans backed down.

Wismer's financial picture turned an ever-deepening shade of red. Only one teller at one branch of the Irving Trust Company was authorized to cash Titan paychecks. As each player submitted his check, the teller subtracted the sum from Wismer's balance. When he reached zero, no more checks were cashed. On pay days, it looked like an all-out blitz on the bank. Some players didn't even change after practice; they threw their coats over their sweat suits and raced down to the bank.

As word of Wismer's indebtedness spread, laundries became leery of Titan checks. As a result, clean socks were available for games only. The Titans needed a set of extra-large shoulder pads for oversized tackle Proverb Jacobs, but were unable to obtain them because sporting goods dealers refused to extend Wismer credit.

Tape ran low, so, like a M.A.S.H. medic, trainer Buddy Leininger was forced to practice triage, setting priorities as to who had the right to be taped first. Backs and ends to the front, linemen to the rear.

Unable to pay for maintenance, Wismer let the locker room decay into the Tobacco Road of pro football. The showers ran cold. The locker room floor was littered with broken glass. The mirrors over the sink became crusted with old shaving cream spelling out obscenities.

Management's lack of professionalism reached ridiculous lows. As the losses mounted on the field, the roster changed radically each Tuesday. New white hopes and black hopes, freshly cut from the NFL or dredged up from some backwater league, arrived at the Polo Grounds. Ed Kovac was cut and rehired five times. But most were nameless fringe players who trooped into the locker room on Tuesday and most often disappeared the following week without a trace.

In a rather bizarre move, Wismer ordered general manager George Sauer to take on the additional duties of the backfield coach. This meant that Sauer was not only the boss of head coach Bulldog Turner, but also Turner's underling.

Wismer ran such a Mickey Mouse operation that the Titans' sole source of draft information was a fifty-cent copy of *Street & Smith's College Football Yearbook*. The rest of the pro teams toted massive dossiers on each graduating senior.

Wismer hindered his club in other ways, making the Titans the last of the one-projector teams. Before each upcoming game, opposing teams exchange game films. One reel shows the opposing team's defensive plays, the other shows its offensive plays. Since the Titans only owned one projector, half the team had to wait in the chilly locker room, dozing, freezing, or shooting craps while the other unit huddled on the floor—there were no chairs—around the faint glow of an old projector. Management's refusal to buy a second projector was an economy measure. When the projector broke down a week before a game in Houston, no one paid to get it fixed. The unprepared Titans lost 56–17.

Money woes continued to mount. At home, the Titans were forced to play on dirt. The Polo Grounds turf had wilted away, and Wismer couldn't afford to replace it or have the groundskeepers do any more than line the field.

The team's publicist apologized to sportswriters for failing to provide post-game statistics. He explained that the supply of mimeographing ink was exhausted along with the Titan funds.

Just before a game in Boston, the driver of the team bus refused to take the Titans to the stadium until he was paid first—in cash. General manager George Sauer came up with the money out of his own pocket.

The 1962 Titans drew only 36,161—not per game, mind you, but for the whole season. To fill the vacant seats, kids in the neighborhood were let in free just before kickoff. It became sort of a tradition for thousands of youngsters to storm through the stands, tripping over the few paid customers. (While the kids on the block sat in 50-yard line seats, the players' wives were seated high in the coffin corner.) By the end of the season, even the lure of free seats failed to attract the kids.

Trying not to look bad, Wismer inflated the attendance figures, but newspapers weren't fooled. "The announced attendance of 20,000 refers to arms and legs," wrote one wag. "Or else 15,000 of the 20,000 people came disguised as empty seats."

For the Titans' final game ever, 2,000 people showed up at the Polo Grounds, but only seventy onlookers were on hand for the final gun in a 44–10 clobbering administered by the Houston Oilers. Maybe the pep talk had something to do with the beating. Five minutes before kickoff, Bulldog Turner had told his troops: "There won't even be any New York Titans next year. So most of you are playing in your last pro game. Most of you aren't good enough to play anywhere else."

PITTSBURGH STEELERS

1955

The Pittsburgh Steelers cut rookie quarterback Johnny Unitas because they said he wasn't smart. History proved it was the Steeler management that wasn't too bright.

Unitas and Vic Eaton were low draft picks fighting for a job as the team's third-string quarterback. Unitas thought he had the edge because he was a local boy and had played against the son of the team owner in a Pittsburgh high school championship game.

But Unitas was not given a minute's playing time during the exhibition season—he was given his walking papers instead. Steeler coach Walt Kiesling explained to owner Art Rooney, "Unitas can't remember the plays. He's too dumb."

Eaton stuck around for just one year and played so infrequently that he threw only twice.

Meanwhile, the Baltimore Colts gave Unitas a chance. He immediately embarked upon a remarkable Hall of Fame career, led the Colts to three championships, and was named the greatest quarterback in the history of the NFL.

ROBERT IRSAY

Owner • Indianapolis (and Baltimore) Colts • 1972–present

Robert Irsay is the laughingstock of the NFL.

Unfortunately, there is nothing funny about his erratic, impulsive interference—meddling that turned the Colts into the Dolts. Since 1972, when Irsay took over the reins of the once proud and mighty Colts, he has single-handedly run the team into the turf. He should be penalized for intentional grounding. His track record speaks for itself: only three winning seasons in the last fourteen years.

Every weekend during the season, Irsay hops in his personal jet and flies to wherever his team is playing. Usually, he screams at the coach— and sometimes the players—before, during, and after each game, and then flies back home to Skokie, Illinois.

Like a rotten, spoiled child, Irsay has made it clear from the very beginning that the team is his toy and he can damn well do with it what he wants. Apparently, that includes wrecking it.

His crude, impetuous intervention has bred nothing but insecurity and chaos on the sidelines. He has already gone through nine coaches— most of whom he dumped because they didn't make good puppets. Irsay just couldn't stand to let his coaches do their jobs.

In the middle of a game in 1974, Irsay grabbed the phone in the owner's box and called coach Howard Schnellenberger, who was coaching on the sidelines. Irsay was incensed because quarterback Marty Domres was playing in place of Bert Jones. "I want Jones in there *now!*" Irsay demanded. In the next series, however, Jones remained on the bench. Within minutes, the angry owner stormed down to the sidelines and confronted his coach. Schnellenberger ordered Irsay to leave the field. Irsay ordered Schnellenberger to look for another job.

Following Irsay's orders—no matter how asinine—didn't help coach Mike McCormack hang on to his job. When the Colts were headed for their tenth straight defeat during a 1981 game, Irsay, again in the owner's box, phoned McCormack on the sidelines. Irsay, who had some friends with him and wanted to show them at least one touchdown, told the coach to alternate quarterbacks on every play and call nothing but passes for the rest of the game. To the shock and anger of the players, the humiliated coach did what he was told (although quarterback Bert Jones did call a couple of running plays to keep his self-respect).

That same year, Irsay stepped even further out of bounds during a game against the Philadelphia Eagles. He started calling plays down to McCormack—including one for an eleven-man blitz! The Colts lost 38–13. And poor McCormack was sacked at the end of the year.

The only coach to ever win for Irsay was Ted Marchibroda. Yet the fatheaded owner made life so miserable for him that Marchibroda resigned in 1977. That prompted the players—who publicly blasted Irsay for destroying the team—to threaten a boycott. Two days later, Irsay rehired Marchibroda. Still in the mood to get rid of somebody, however, Irsay fired general manager Joe Thomas.

In 1983, Irsay made a fool out of coach Frank Kush. The imprudent owner traded away the Colts' No. 1 draft choice, John Elway, without even informing Kush. Kush resigned the following year.

Irsay treated his players with the same madness that he displayed to his coaches. He reached the heights of lunacy in his handling of kicker Toni Linhart. Linhart had missed an easy field goal (one of his 3 failed attempts that day) that cost the Colts the game. In the locker room afterward, Linhart was glumly sitting alone when Irsay came over and patted him on the back. Irsay told him, "I'm going to give you a $10,000 bonus." But later that week, Irsay gave Linhart something else—his outright release.

Irsay traded away or gave walking papers to many beloved players, including running back Lydell Mitchell, the only Colt ever to rush for more than 1,000 yards in a season. After Mitchell came to contract terms with the team's general manager, Irsay aborted the deal the next day by trading Mitchell, outraging Baltimore fans. Irsay proved he was a public relations bozo when he fired Lenny Moore from his job as the team's community relations director; Irsay waited until the middle of the 1982 football strike—when the sport was at its lowest ebb—to can the Hall of Famer.

"We don't have to knock Irsay," a Baltimore sportswriter once said. "All we have to do is describe exactly what he does and everyone can see he's an ass."

That was never made clearer than in the spring of 1984. Irsay threatened to move his team unless he received all sorts of concessions from the City of Baltimore and the State of Maryland. The mayor and the governor agreed to his demands—but Irsay had no intention of staying. All the while he was secretly negotiating with Indianapolis, which desperately wanted a team. He extorted from Indianapolis $7 million in guaranteed annual revenues for each of twelve years; a $12.5 million loan; a $4 million training facility, and use of the Hoosier Dome, a 61,000-seat indoor stadium.

Irsay followed his typical modus operandi and spirited the Colts out of town under cover of darkness. In the wee hours of March 29, 1984, Irsay sneaked fifteen moving vans into the Colts' training facility in Owings Mills, Maryland. Once they were loaded up, the vans skulked toward Indianapolis, putting an end to Baltimore's 31-year stay in pro football. Irsay didn't even call the mayor to say good-bye.

The shock of Baltimore fans hadn't worn off yet when Indianapolis fans received their first jolt from Irsay. At a gathering of new Colts boosters, Irsay revealed his true colors by tactlessly announcing to the cordial crowd, "It's not *your* team. It's not *our* team. It's *my family's* team. I paid for it."

Back in Baltimore, a sympathetic former fan said, "With the Colts, you get Irsay. And the people of Indianapolis are going to regret that they ever met him." They already have.

BUD ADAMS

Owner ▪ Houston Oilers ▪ 1966

Bud Adams had this great idea—Operation Crosscheck. Like a prospector scouting a worked-over mine, Adams decided to scan all the colleges, large and small, for potential rookies that the other pro teams had missed. Convinced he would discover a gem or two, he invited more than 100 overlooked graduates to the Oiler training camp.

He also invited nothing but trouble. The chagrined owner soon found out why the rest of the league had ignored these collegians.

In the group of hopefuls were more butterfingers, cream puffs, and fruit cakes than you'd find at a sweet shop counter. Working out in shorts because there weren't enough uniforms to go around, the prospects impressed no one but themselves. After only four practice sessions, Oiler coach Wally Lemm made his first cuts. He didn't have time to give the bad news to each player individually, so he cut them by the busload.

Among the Crosscheck players trying out for the team were a South American waiter who wanted to be a kicker and a 6-foot, 10-inch basketball player from Texas Tech who was so tall he couldn't bend down far enough to hit the blocking sled.

Of the 126 Crosscheck prospects whom Adams had invited to camp, not a single one survived the final cut. But two did get Adams' undivided attention: they sued him because they didn't make the team!

HALFTIME HORRORS

There's a reason why it's called the halftime show. No matter how dreadful the game is after two quarters, half the time the show is worse. NFL clubs tend to feature productions as entertaining as Army training films. Schools, on the other hand, often present marching bands in routines so gross they make rock videos seem like kiddie fare. For "The Most Tasteless Halftime Shows," The Football Hall of SHAME inducts the following:

STANFORD MARCHING BAND

"Tribute to Presidential Diseases" • Sept. 14, 1985

While the nation sent get-well cards to President Reagan after his cancer surgery, the Stanford marching band went one better—or worse, depending on your point of view. It performed a halftime show called "Tribute to Presidential Diseases."

First, the band paid homage to the removal of a cyst on Reagan's nose. Part of the band marched onto the field and formed a giant nose with a bump on it. Then, to the tune of "A Crazy Little Thing Called Love," another group of band members formed huge pincers that squeezed the nose until the cyst popped out.

For its next routine, the band made two big dots to form a gigantic colon—the punctuation mark. "It was supposed to represent the President's colon, but it may have been too subtle for a lot of the fans," said band manager Jeff Stephens. The colon on the field turned into a semi colon as the band played "One at a Time." That tune was chosen, said Stephens, with the logic typical of an underclassman, "because the surgeons removed only one part of Reagan's colon at a time, I guess."

For the finale, the band spelled out "BENIGN" on the field while playing the song "Kick It Out."

If anything deserved to be diagnosed as sick, it was this crass performance.

COLUMBIA MARCHING BAND

"Birth Control" • Oct. 28, 1967

The Columbia marching band abandoned the oompah of old to comment on a major sociological development of our time—the birth control pill.

To many fans, however, it was hard to conceive of a more indecorous halftime show.

During its routine at a home game, the irreverent band honored the Pill by forming a giant calendar and playing "I Got Rhythm"—a song the band audaciously dedicated to the Vatican.

After a pregnant pause, the band bred further resentment when it formed the outline of a shotgun and played "Get Me to the Church on Time."

The Columbia band had actually prepared the show for a game at Dartmouth, but officials there aborted the birth control script.

RICE UNIVERSITY BAND

Aggie Spoof • Nov. 17, 1973

Occasionally a marching band can hold the audience captive. Unfortunately for Rice, the reverse was true. The audience held the band captive.

Members of the Rice marching band, known as "The Mob," were foolish enough to think they could mock the Texas A & M Aggies and get away with it. At the time, A & M was a spit-and-polish, all-male military academy very proud of its precision marching band. It stood for all that was right with the good ol' U.S. of A. Like motherhood and apple pie, it was something you just didn't parody.

So with total disregard for their own safety, The Mob decided to poke fun at the A & M band during a home game against the Aggies at Rice Stadium in Houston. The Rice musicians wore dirty, ragged old Army fatigues as they staggered out of step onto the field. The Mob's drum major led the way—doing the German goosestep.

The unamused cadets booed and jeered. But they were set to wage war when Rice had the effrontery to satirize A & M's beloved mascot, Reveille, an American collie that ran up and down the sidelines barking at rival bands and teams. He was really a nuisance, but the Aggies loved him and, as The Mob soon discovered, woe be to those who made fun of him. In its routine, the band formed a giant puddle around a dummy fire hydrant and played "Oh Where, Oh Where Has My Little Dog Gone."

That did it. A squad of enraged cadets launched a sneak attack on the band in the middle of its performance. Leaping from the stands, the ambushers shoved several musicians to the turf before escaping into a cheering Aggie crowd.

After the band members finished the show and returned to their seats, hundreds of irate cadets pelted them with litter. At the end of the game—won by underdog Rice 24–20—the band was held under siege by the hostile cadets. For nearly two hours, 200 or so uniformed Aggies swarmed outside the stadium while the band members, under police protection, huddled below the south end-zone seats.

When two dozen cops couldn't disperse the hot-headed cadets, one Mobster muttered, "I can't believe this is America. Here we are surrounded in our own stadium by Aggies!"

Despite his cry for freedom, the Mobster—and all his cohorts— could only escape the Aggies by stealth; they were smuggled out, four and five at a time, in food service trucks.

SAN FRANCISCO POLICE DEPARTMENT

Gestapo Family Reunion • Aug. 19, 1973

A special halftime show at Candlestick Park was supposed to be a salute to the friendly neighborhood policeman, the cheerful cop who finds lost children, helps old ladies across the street, and returns bicycles swiped by bullies.

But fans attending the preseason game between the San Francisco 49ers and the San Diego Chargers were horrified by the poor taste of the production—it looked like a get-together of SS madman Heinrich Himmler and his troops.

A squadron of helicopters droned overhead while a fleet of police cars roared into the stadium, sirens screaming and red lights spinning madly. Suddenly, a car with the word "kidnapper" painted on the side drove into view. That was the cue for the good guys in blue to chase after the bad guys in black.

Guns blazed away. (Thank God, the cops used blanks.) Police dogs snarled. A German shepherd dragged one of the "criminals" about ten yards, as if he were a rag doll.

About the only things the San Francisco police assaulted were the sensitivities of the crowd. Moaned one off-duty police sergeant, "There goes our image again! Why do they have to show the violence? I mean, everybody knows that's the dirty end of our job. But there are so many other things the police do to serve. Tomorrow there will be 59,602 more people muttering about police brutality."

To cap off the exhibition, actor Karl Malden, who at the time was starring in the hit TV cop show "The Streets of San Francisco," told the fans that the policeman was their friend. Fans began to think "With friends like these who needs enemies?"

UNIVERSITY OF VIRGINIA MARCHING BAND

"Family Feud" • Nov. 2, 1985

West Virginians sure don't cotton to no strangers pokin' fun at their wimmenfolk an' their state. Why, dang it all, the Virginia marchin' band plum went too far in razzin' West Virginia—and on national tellyvision to boot.

The good people of the Mountaineer State had a right to fume. They were cruelly mocked by the Award Winning University of Virginia Fighting Cavalier Indoor/Outdoor Precision Marching Pep Band and Chowder Society Revue Unlimited.

At halftime during the Virginia–West Virginia clash, the band parodied the TV game show "Family Feud," pitting the hillbilly Hatfields of West Virginia against the upstanding Fenwicks of Virginia.

In the show, the Richard Dawson impersonator gave "Maw" Hatfield a quick peck on the cheek and asked her, "What do you associate with the state of West Virginia?" Maw answered, "Fine education." The forty members of the band formed a large "X" on the field and a loud buzz came over the P.A. system, indicating an incorrect answer.

Next up was Uncle Jed, and his answer about his native state was, "All the wimmenfolk are on birth control." Again, the band formed an "X" and the buzzer sounded.

Finally, it was up to Cousin Zack to save the Hatfields from elimination. He answered, "Indoor plumbing." But he too was wrong, and that meant the Hatfields had struck out.

At that point, the Dawson character turned to the Fenwicks. Biff Fenwick, a strapping lad, was asked to name something he associated with West Virginia. He replied, "This sounds tacky, but . . . toxic gas." He was alluding to recent alerts at Union Carbide plants.

Said the Dawson double, "Our survey says . . ." and the band formed the number 100. "In the No. 1 answer, 100 out of 100 surveyed said 'toxic gas.' "

Needless to say, the West Virginia fans sitting in Virginia's Scott Stadium were not amused. In fact, State Treasurer A. James Manchin was so upset that he sent letters of protest to Virginia's governor and both senators—and even evoked the name of one of our country's founding fathers.

Wrote Manchin: "Thomas Jefferson would surely hang his head in shame at the actions of his university for such callousness and egregious lies and distortions unleashed by a so-called institution of higher learning."

Jefferson would have held one truth to be self-evident—that the Virginia band did not have the unalienable right to besmirch the good name of the State of West Virginia.

ZEBRA ZEROES

Referees are part of the game, like fumbles, losing streaks, and missed blocks. Without them, what would fans have to complain about? Grudgingly, fans must admit that referees are pretty honest fellows. It's just that the men in the zebra shirts aren't always right. You'd swear that some of their calls were made from the bottom of a huge pileup. For "The Most Flagrantly Blown Calls by Referees," The Football Hall of SHAME inducts the following:

TOM LOUTTIT

Dec. 5, 1936

Referees are not allowed to take sides in a game. But ref Tom Louttit did. He actually ran interference for a ball carrier.

On one incredible play, Louttit acted as a twelfth man for the University of Southern California Trojans during their annual tussle with the Notre Dame Fighting Irish.

Late in the first half with the score tied 6–all, the Irish drove down to the USC 9-yard line. But on the next play, Trojan defender Bud Langley intercepted a pass on the 2-yard line and began to sprint upfield. He spurted past all his blockers and thought he was alone until he saw, out of the corner of his eye, that Louttit was running beside him stride for stride.

Louttit, being the ever-vigilant referee, was determined to stay on top of the play. But he didn't even bother to notice Notre Dame fullback Larry Danbom thundering down the field from the flank, making 2 yards to Langley's one. At the Irish 20-yard line, Danbom was going for the tackle when Louttit smacked into him and took him out of the play. The ref had just neatly blocked out the only man with a chance of catching the runner.

Meanwhile, Langley trotted untouched into the end zone for a lucky 98-yard interception return. It was a crucial play because the game ended in a 13–13 tie.

One drunken Irish rooter charged down from the stands after Louttit's perfect block. When the Trojans lined up for the extra point attempt, the lush shouted at the ref, "As long as you gave the Trojans a touchdown, the least you could do is block the kick!"

NORM SCHACHTER   JOE CONNELL   BURL TOLER
JACK FETTE   ADRIAN BURK   GEORGE ELLIS
Dec. 8, 1968

Jesse James and his gang would have been proud to have pulled off such a job. In front of millions of network TV viewers, referee Norm Schachter and his crew robbed the Los Angeles Rams of a crucial down—a crime that cost the team a shot at the Western Division title.

It was the biggest game of the year for the Rams. A win against the visiting Chicago Bears would put L.A. only ½ game behind the first-place Baltimore Colts and set the stage for a Rams–Colts showdown the following week in the final game of the regular season.

But Chicago played tough and held a 17–16 lead with 35 seconds left in the game. The Rams, however, were on the Bears' 32-yard line—within range of a winning field goal.

On first down, L.A. quarterback Roman Gabriel threw an incomplete pass. Rams lineman Charley Cowan was detected holding so the Bears accepted a penalty, a devastating one that pushed the Rams back 21 yards (15 yards from the point of the infraction). Since the down remained the same on the penalty, it was now first-and-31 on the Rams' own 47-yard line.

At least it was supposed to be first down. Unaccountably, the official marker on the sideline read second down. Even worse, none of the officials bothered to correct the obvious error. The Rams were making such a frantic bid to score that they failed to notice they had been short-changed of a vital down. Gabriel then threw three straight incompletions. Although it now should have been fourth down, Schachter signaled first-and-10 for the Bears. Chicago then ran out the clock to win.

Sportswriters and fans weren't the only ones who realized the Rams had been deprived of a fourth-down play. NFL Commissioner Pete Rozelle realized it, too. In a move unprecedented in professional football, Rozelle suspended Schachter and his crew for the remainder of the year without pay.

That did little to pacify the Rams. They still lost the game—and a chance at the championship.

BILL HALLORAN

Dec. 3, 1939

As Washington Redskins placekicker Bo Russell waited for the snap, there was no doubt in the minds of the 62,404 fans at the Polo Grounds that the Redskins were about to win the Eastern Division.

Although they trailed the New York Giants 9–7 with less than a minute remaining, the Redskins were lined up at the 11-yard line for an easy chip shot that would give them a 10–9 victory and the title.

The snap and placement were perfect, and Russell booted the ball in a high arc toward the right goal post. The players stopped charging and blocking and turned to watch the flight of the ball. Once it cleared the goal post, the Redskins began jumping up and down, congratulating each other. Several Giants slammed down their helmets in despair.

New York captain Mel Hein, seeing one of the Redskins hesitate, said, "What are you waiting for? It was good. Now go back and kick off."

Even Giants tackle Ed Widseth, who had punched Washington's end Johnny Spirida two plays earlier, grabbed Spirida's hand, shook it, and said, "Congratulations, Johnny. You guys played a swell game and deserved to win."

The Redskins may have deserved to win, but they didn't. Long after the ball had sailed into the end-zone seats, referee Bill Halloran started to raise his hands to signal good, but then, incredibly, ruled otherwise.

To their happy surprise, the Giants realized that Halloran had just handed them a 9–7 victory and the division title.

The Washington players were stunned. Then they began jumping up and down again—this time in outrage. Their coach, Ray Flaherty, leaped off the bench and charged after Halloran. "What do you mean, 'No good'?" the coach screamed. "Everyone in the stadium knows it was good, including the Giants."

"It could have gone either way," replied Halloran, who, more than any other man, knew exactly how General Custer felt when he was surrounded by angry Redskins.

In an uncontrollable outburst, Washington back Ed Justice, never known to argue with an official before, tore after Halloran. He was nearly blackjacked by a New York policeman before being dragged away by a teammate. Meanwhile, upset fans spilled onto the field to voice their protests. It took 5 minutes to clear the field—and another half an hour after the game to break up all the fights in the stands.

Halloran's horrendously bad call was the second he had made against Washington in two weeks. When the Redskins tried a field goal against the Detroit Lions the week before, Halloran ruled the kick wide. After the game, he admitted to Coach Flaherty that he had blown the call—that the kick had looked good.

But in both cases, Halloran's wrong call couldn't be changed. One thing *was* changed—his status in the NFL. Following the title game, Redskins owner George Marshall managed to get Halloran banned as a league referee.

The next day, Flaherty, still smarting from the loss, said, "If that guy has a conscience, he'll never have another good night's sleep as long as he lives."

RED FRIESELL

Nov. 16, 1940

In one of the dumbest officiating blunders in football history, referee Red Friesell allowed a team to score the winning touchdown on a fifth down.

Friesell revealed his shocking lack of math skills in a game between the Cornell Big Red and the Dartmouth Big Green in Hanover, New Hampshire. Rated No. 1 in the nation, Cornell was riding an 18-game winning streak when it faced Dartmouth, a two-touchdown underdog.

Confounding the experts and the bookies, Dartmouth played inspired football, and was holding a slim 3–0 lead with only a minute to play in the game when Cornell drove down to the Dartmouth 6-yard line. The Dartmouth defense stiffened, and Cornell failed to score on 3 running plays and an incomplete pass.

The Big Green fans and players jumped for joy. Only 3 seconds remained and it was Dartmouth's ball. Or was it? Counting like a preschooler, Friesell signaled it was *fourth* down for Cornell and placed the ball on the 6-yard line. Dartmouth's protests fell on deaf ears.

Incomprehensibly, none of the other three officials questioned Friesell's boneheaded ruling.

Given a surprise gift, Cornell lined up for an unprecedented fifth down. On the final play of the game, quarterback Walt Scholl lofted a pass to halfback Bill Murphy in the end zone to record a dramatic, but tainted, 7–3 victory.

Throughout the night, the town of Hanover seethed. The officials were burned in effigy. Films of the game showed beyond a shadow of a doubt that Friesell had erred.

Cornell had won illegally. But to its credit, the school gave up the victory three days later and graciously declared that Dartmouth had won the game, 3–0. Only the bookies refused to accept the change.

Despite committing a boner that made headlines across America, Friesell was sought after by many coaches. Ohio State's Francis Schmidt, whose team was trounced 40–0 by Michigan, wired Friesell: "WISH YOU HAD WORKED OUR GAME SATURDAY. WE NEEDED SOMETHING." Ducky Pond, coach of Yale, which was drubbed 28–0 by Harvard that same afternoon, telegrammed the referee: "ENTIRE STUDENT BODY BREATHLESSLY AWAITING WORD FROM YOU REGARDING HARVARD GAME. DID WE REALLY LOSE? CAN'T YOU DO SOMETHING FOR US?"

Friesell had been ridiculed enough and deserved a little compassion. So what did conference commissioner Asa Bushnell do? He wired the beleaguered official: "DON'T LET IT GET YOU DOWN, DOWN, DOWN, DOWN, DOWN."

BOOING THE BOOSTERS

Fans come to the stadium to watch a game and engage in one of America's favorite pastimes—booing—at the whistle-happy ref, the fumble-fingered runner, the color-blind passer. But sometimes the real boos shouldn't be directed toward the playing field but right up in the stands, where fans have displayed some of the rudest, raunchiest, rowdiest conduct this side of a riot zone. For "The Most Unruly Behavior of Fans," The Football Hall of SHAME inducts the following:

THE SNOWBALLER

Denver Broncos Fan • Nov. 11, 1985

A dunderheaded fan in Denver's Mile High Stadium pulled a witless grandstand play that cost the San Francisco 49ers a victory.

He was the first fan to throw a snowball that directly affected the outcome of a professional football game.

The icy missile splattered on the field right in front of 49ers place-holder Matt Cavanaugh a split second before he tried to spot the ball for a 19-yard field goal attempt by Ray Wersching at the end of the first half. Distracted, Cavanaugh muffed the snap and was unable to put the ball down for Wersching. Cavanaugh then scrambled with the ball and lofted a desperation pass that fell incomplete. It was a crucial play because San Francisco lost to the Denver Broncos by only one point, 17–16.

The Snowballer had taken his cue from a group of tanked up fans who thought they could help ice the game for their Broncos by flinging snowballs onto the field. They had already nailed 49er quarterback Joe Montana in the huddle. And when side judge Bill Quinby lay sprawled and hurt on the ground after colliding with a player, the fans showed their concern by pelting him with a barrage of snowballs.

Although at least fifty fans were ejected from the stadium for throwing snowballs during the nationally televised Monday night game, only the Snowballer attained instant notoriety—and shame.

"It just happened on the spur of the moment," he confessed later. "Me and my buddy both threw snowballs at the same time. His hit the left upright [of the north goal post] and mine bounced in front of Cavanaugh."

Cavanaugh confirmed that the snowball had distracted him and caused him to bobble the snap. "It landed right about the time the ball was snapped," he said. "It took my mind off the ball and I dropped it."

It was a hell of a throw. The snowball flew at least 35 yards from Section 17 to the ground in front of Cavanaugh. But the Snowballer couldn't enjoy his accuracy. "Everybody around us started calling us jerks," he said. "That's when I realized it was stupid."

Just who would be that stupid? That's what *The San Francisco Examiner* wanted to know. In a questionable example of checkbook journalism, the newspaper offered $500 for the Snowballer to step forward and tell his story. He did, but declined to reveal his name or accept the money.

"I'm really sorry about what I did and I want to apologize to the 49ers and the 49er fans," he told *The Examiner*. "I don't want the money. I feel bad enough already. Everybody thinks I'm a jerk."

Can you blame them?

DONALD ENNIS

Baltimore Colts Fan • Dec. 11, 1971

Of all the fans who ever raced onto the gridiron to snatch the ball during a game, Donald Ennis ranks as the most foolhardy.

He actually tried to swipe the pigskin from right under the nose of Baltimore Colts linebacker Mike Curtis, one of the fiercest barbarians in pro football.

Ennis, a bespectacled 30-year-old lightweight from Rochester, New York, was behaving like a typical fan during a Colts' home game against the Miami Dolphins. Suddenly, Ennis was seized with an uncontrollable urge to run onto the field and grab the football—the one Curtis and colleagues were playing with.

Everyone who valued life and limb knew better than to mess with Curtis. Apparently, Ennis didn't fully appreciate the reasons why Curtis was called "The Animal." Hadn't Ennis heard the stories? The ones about how Curtis ate the window panes of the team bus on the way to games; how he chewed the bars right off his face guard; how during a practice scrimmage he beat up the opposing center—who just happened to be his roommate; and how he mauled his own quarterback, the revered Johnny Unitas, in practice.

Obviously, Ennis was not an informed fan. With about 3 minutes left in the game, Ennis left his end-zone seat and vaulted onto the field just as the Colts were breaking from their defensive huddle on the 40-yard line. He scooped up the ball and raced for the sideline. "What the hell's going on here?" thundered Curtis.

With the dispatch of an irate 6-foot, 4-inch, 235-pound linebacker, Curtis tore after the interloper. Catching up with Ennis, Curtis removed the ball from his hands—the hard way. While 60,000 Municipal Stadium fans winced, Curtis swung his padded forearm and whacked Ennis with a vicious smash to the neck—a blow that, in a game, would have brought a 15-yard penalty for unnecessary roughness. "Welcome to the National Football League," growled Curtis. Ennis dropped the ball and dropped to the ground, unconscious.

When he was revived, Ennis was taken to the hospital, and then to the Baltimore Municipal Court Building, where he was charged with disorderly conduct.

After the game, Curtis said, "I believe in law and order. That fellow had no right being on the field. I felt it was in line to make him aware of his wrongdoing."

Ennis had plenty of time to think about his wrongdoing. He spent the next two weeks recovering in bed.

NEW ENGLAND PATRIOTS FANS

Oct. 19, 1976

It was a sorry night for football. Late on a fall evening in 1976, the game degenerated into a disgusting spectacle of unnecessary roughness, illegal use of hands, senseless injuries, and countless fist fights. Not on the field. In the stands.

In what has become known as the Monday Night Massacre, hooliganism reigned at Schaefer Stadium in Foxboro, Massachusetts during a game between the New England Patriots and the visiting New York Jets.

Because the game started at 9 P.M., a tough, young crowd had had plenty of time before the kickoff to get crocked. They stayed juiced, too; beer sold briskly inside the stadium, which, incidentally, had been named after a brewery.

Under cover of darkness, the place really went up for grabs. Throughout the game, drunks and young punks roamed in and around the stadium. One youth grabbed a policeman's gun and waved it in the air, yelling, "Come and get me!" The cops did. Brawls broke out in section after section, a police officer's jaw was busted, and an elderly woman was hit in the head with a bottle. It got so bad that some imbecilic jerk actually stole a wheelchair out from under a handicapped person. Even more loathsome was a drunken fan who urinated on a medic's back as the medic administered mouth-to-mouth resuscitation to a heart attack victim under the stands.

The obnoxious behavior spilled down onto the field, where the Pats were routing the Jets 41–7. The home team fought off a host of boozed-up fans, who had decided it would be fun to run onto the field during the game. Police and ushers dragged a dozen of the rowdies off to the pokey, where they joined another fifty or so who had been arrested for other crimes. Because the paddywagons couldn't haul them away fast enough, some of the overenthusiastic fans were handcuffed to the chain-link fence surrounding the stadium while awaiting transportation to jail.

Apparently, the fans didn't learn their lesson. Four years later, on September 29, 1980, when the Patriots hosted the Denver Broncos, the stadium was rocked by another night of horror.

Because the game hadn't been sold out in time to avert a TV blackout, there was a last-minute rush to buy tickets. When the lines failed to move quickly, angry patrons stormed the understaffed ticket booths.

Meanwhile, a monstrous traffic jam along U.S. Route 1—the only access to the stadium—prompted many fans to leave their cars a mile or more away and walk toward the stadium along the poorly lighted roadway. Many fans didn't reach their seats until halftime. When they arrived, they found youths tossing cups of beer at one another, flinging Frisbees at near-decapitation velocity, and throwing fists in scuffles.

As cops swept into the stands to make arrests, they were booed and doused with beer and mustard. One policeman was kicked in the back during a fracas and was rushed to the hospital. Outside, youths rampaged through the parking lots, snapping off auto antennas, kicking in car doors, and urinating on tires.

Exiting traffic was so backed up that some fans didn't get out of the parking lot for more than two hours. Bonfires were built, and drinking and fighting continued until the wee hours of Tuesday morning. When dawn broke, police had tallied forty-nine arrests.

Proving that the Patriots fans deserved to be the league leaders in spectator rowdyism, a *Boston Globe* reporter who sat in the stands for a game at Schaefer Stadium wrote a detailed account of "lewd remarks made to women in the parking lot, sodden men urinating into restroom sinks, people vomiting in the aisles, shirtless celebrants with sagging bellies, beer being spilled on neighbors, obscene shouts at Patriot players and gynecological suggestions directed at their cheerleaders, drunken brawls in the parking lot and beer-swilling males packed six to a car knocking down highway cones on the way home." And that was on a typical Sunday afternoon!

IOWA HAWKEYES FANS

Nov. 24, 1905

Fans have often been loud enough to drive opposing teams batty, but no rooters were as noisy as Iowa's engineering students.

For the Hawkeyes' game against the rival Iowa State Cyclones, the students tinkered all week in preparation of a tremendous surprise. On the day of the game, they carted out their prize noisemaker—an old steam engine that emitted a piercing three-tone whistle.

Wearing cotton in their ears, the engineers set up the whistle on the south end of the grandstand. Then, every time the Cyclones had the ball, the fans tied down the cord to the whistle and blasted the daylights out of Iowa State.

The helmet-rattling blare was so loud that none of the Cyclones could hear the quarterback. He was forced to go from player to player shouting the signals. But that did little good. The racket disrupted their timing and broke their concentration. Needless to say, only a few tiny peeps were sounded when the ball was in Iowa's possession. Iowa won 8–0.

After the game, authorities confiscated the deafening noisemaker and it was never heard from again.

TENNESSEE MOUNTAINEER

Tennessee Volunteers Fan • Oct. 24, 1908

While most fans are content to shoot off their mouths, one Tennessee fan went too far. He wanted to shoot off his revolver—at the Georgia Bulldogs.

It happened in Knoxville, where the Bulldogs had to battle not only the Tennessee Volunteers but the unruly spectators as well.

Georgia coach Steadman Sanford was constantly harassed on the sidelines by a nasty group of Tennessee fans, who crowded around him, taunting and ridiculing him throughout the game. One of his tormentors was a grizzled mountaineer reeking of sour mash and dressed in a frock coat and wide-brimmed hat.

With the game scoreless midway in the first half, Georgia marched down to the Tennessee 2-yard line. While the alarmed Vols fans shouted words of encouragement to the defense, the mountaineer casually strode on to the field and up to the Georgia huddle. Fingering a .38 revolver, he pointed it toward the goal line. "The first man who crosses that line," he drawled menacingly at the Bulldogs, "will get a bullet in his carcass."

The mountaineer was hustled away by police, but not before he had made his point. Georgia fumbled on the next play and Tennessee recovered. After that threat, the Bulldogs never got close to the end zone the rest of the day, and lost 10–0.

BALTIMORE COLTS FANS

Dec. 12, 1948

No pro football spectators were more enraged by an official's questionable call than the Baltimore Colts fans. They were so out of control they made the days of the lawless Wild West seem like the days of wine and roses.

With blood in their eyes and vengeance in their hearts, the Colts fans actually formed a posse and set out to apprehend and lynch the man who had "robbed" their team of victory.

During most of the game, there was no hint that mob rule would prevail at Baltimore's Stadium. The Colts were holding on to a 17–14 fourth-quarter lead over the Buffalo Bills in the play-off for the Eastern Division title of the All-American Football Conference.

Then came the hotly disputed play. Bills' halfback Chet Mutryn appeared to catch a short pass, take three steps, and then drop the ball as he was tackled. The ball was recovered by the Colts. Head linesman Tommy Whelan, however, ruled the play an incomplete pass. Irate fans screamed in protest for the rest of the game—and went crazy 6 plays after the call when the Bills scored the winning touchdown.

The bang from the gun signaled the end of the game and the beginning of the mob's search-and-destroy mission. About 1,000 fans swarmed onto the field, harassing the officials in the hunt for Whelan. The first few goons in the posse to find Whelan knocked him down and kicked him.

Realizing he had no chance of defending himself, players from both teams came to Whelan's rescue. But not before he had suffered a swollen eye, a ripped shirt, and a torn cap in the beating. He and the other officials were escorted into the stadium's administration building and extra police were called out to thwart any attempt by the mob to storm the place.

Fans threw bottles and garbage on the playing field and surrounded the building. They refused to disperse. Whelan managed to escape by being smuggled out of the stadium and into the Buffalo Bills' team bus.

When the fans learned that their prey had given them the slip, they were so burned up they set fire to some of the west side seats. Their blaze was doused; their ire was not.

CALVIN COOLIDGE

President • United States of America • Dec. 7, 1925

If Calvin Coolidge had known as much about politics as he did about football, he never would have made it to the White House.

The thirtieth president of the United States showed what kind of football fan he was when Illinois Senator William McKinley arranged for Coolidge to meet Red Grange. No athlete was more popular at the time than Grange, the Galloping Ghost. After starring for the University of Illinois, Grange had signed an unprecedented six-figure contract to play for the Chicago Bears.

In 1924, Grange turned college football on its ear in a game against the University of Michigan. In the first 12 minutes, he ran back the opening kickoff 95 yards for a touchdown, and went on to score on runs of 67, 56, and 44 yards. He added another TD later in the game to cap one of the greatest individual performances in football history. When Grange joined the Bears, he was instrumental in launching professional football to the heights it has reached today.

The day before his meeting with Coolidge, Grange played in front of 65,000 fans at the Polo Grounds in New York. He scored a touchdown and intercepted a pass, helping the Bears whip the Giants 14–7 in a game covered by such illustrious writers as Grantland Rice, Westbrook Pegler, and Damon Runyon.

By now, everyone in America had heard of Red Grange. Well, almost everyone.

McKinley's limousine brought Grange to the White House. There, the senator introduced the football star to Coolidge. "Mr. President," said McKinley, "this is Red Grange of the Chicago Bears." Coolidge shook Grange's hand and said, quite seriously, "Nice to meet you, young man. I've always liked animal acts."

FLORIDA GATORS FANS

June, 1985

A group of Gator boosters decided to give defrocked coach Charley Pell just what they thought he deserved after he landed the Florida football program in the NCAA jailhouse. Did they publicly condemn him? Did they demand his resignation? Nope. They bought him a shiny, new $24,000 car!

Because Pell violated literally hundreds of recruiting regulations, he cloaked the state's largest university in a shroud of shame. The football team was stripped of its 1984 Southeastern Conference title, placed on probation, and banned from any live TV coverage and bowl games for two years.

The stunned and chagrined university administration promptly fired Pell. Most Gator fans were outraged by the coach's illegal and distasteful recruiting practices and backed the school's actions.

A bunch of benevolent moneybags, however, were outraged, too—by Pell's firing. In a classic case of misguided loyalty, about two dozen of these imprudent souls—including New York Yankees owner George Steinbrenner—chipped in $1,000 each to buy good ol' Charley a brand-new Lincoln Town Car.

And who says crime doesn't pay?

THE LEAPER

Boston Patriots Fan • Nov. 3, 1961

Most spectators are involved in the game. But one fan was too involved—he killed a team's chance for victory by deflecting a would-be touchdown pass. Worse yet, he got away with it.

In the closing moments of an AFL clash between the visiting Dallas Texans (forerunners of the Kansas City Chiefs) and the Boston Patriots, the Texans were trailing 28–21 when they attempted a last-ditch flea flicker. The pass sailed 70 yards and was caught by Chris Burford, who fought off three defenders and fell on the Boston 3-yard line.

Thousands of eager Patriots fans, thinking the game was over, ran onto the field. But the referees said there was time for one more play. The spectators were hustled off the field but allowed to ring the end zone. Somehow, one rabid rooter managed to slip unnoticed into the Patriot secondary.

Before the fan was detected, Dallas quarterback Cotton Davidson took the snap and fired a pass to Burford in the end zone. The ball never reached the receiver. Instead, the fan-turned-defender leaped into the air and tipped the ball away as the final gun sounded. Then he disappeared into the cheering crowd.

Incredibly, in all the confusion, none of the officials spotted the fan's interference. None of the Texans did either, except for Davidson. But his cries of protest fell on deaf ears. Even his own coach, Hank Stram, wouldn't listen to him.

When film of the game was developed, however, there was no dispute— the camera had caught the fan in the act of deflecting the pass and ruining the Texans' bid for a game-saving touchdown.

No one knows for sure who the Leaper was. But, says Patriots spokesman Dave Loftis, with tongue in cheek, "The legend has grown around here that it was really [Patriots owner] Billy Sullivan."

TOILET BOWLS

Bowl games aren't always all that they are cracked up to be. Naturally, the promoters want everyone to believe that the post-season classics showcase the nation's best teams—with dazzling touchdown passes, thrilling broken-field running, and bone-crunching hits. But sometimes these long-awaited events deserve to be flushed into the sewer of disgrace. For "The Most Atrocious Bowl Game Performances," The Football Hall of SHAME inducts the following:

ROSE BOWL

Jan. 1, 1923

The 1923 Rose Bowl game left a thorn in the side of football purists.

Before the game between Penn State and the University of Southern California even started, the two head coaches squared off for a fight on the 50-yard line.

The game was scheduled to begin at 2:15 P.M., but by 2:30 P.M., Penn State still had not shown up. The crowd of 50,000 fidgeted in the hot California sun while Trojan coach "Gloomy Gus" Henderson paced nervously up and down the sideline.

When the tardy Nittany Lions finally showed up, Henderson marched to midfield and confronted Penn State coach Hugo Bezdek.

"Where have you been?" Henderson asked.

"We got caught in a traffic jam trying to get out here," explained Bezdek.

Henderson shook his head and angrily declared, "You were stalling so we'd get itchy and lose our fine fighting edge. And besides, you wanted the sun lower, believing you'd have a better chance when it's cool."

"You're a lot of bunk!" snapped Bezdek.

"You're a liar!" shouted Henderson.

"Go ahead," said Bezdek. "Take off your glasses."

Henderson reached for his glasses. But then he remembered that Bezdek had earned his way through college fighting as a pro boxer under an assumed name. Figuring that discretion was the better part of valor, Henderson said, "Suppose we let the teams settle the issue."

The ensuing Rose Bowl game might as well have been a back-alley fight, complete with black eyes and flying elbows. The game ended in darkness, but all was bright for Henderson; his Trojans won 14–3.

Bezdek was so angry he barred the press from his locker room. When the sore loser finally consented to interviews, he lambasted California. "It isn't the heat out here so much," he said. "It's the humanity."

ORANGE BOWL

Jan. 2, 1939

This wasn't a bowl game; it was a brawl game. The color scheme should have been changed from orange to red for all the blood that was spilled. It looked like college football's version of the Hatfields and McCoys.

In the roughest, no-holds-barred bowl game ever played, the Tennessee Volunteers and Oklahoma Sooners threw fists and curses on almost every play. When the final gun sounded the cease-fire, 25 penalties had been called, including 9 for unnecessary roughness. Officials marched off an Orange Bowl record of 221 yards in penalties (130 against Tennessee and 91 against Oklahoma).

The game (won by the Vols 17–0) turned into a knock-down-drag-out battle on the very first play. Tennessee tailback George Cafego blocked Oklahoma's All-America end Waddy Young with a devastating blow that sent the Sooner sprawling—and out of the game. In retaliation, Vols' blocking back Sam Bartholomew had his nose broken by a well-aimed fist. From then on, the rugged boys from the hills and farms attempted, with bone-crushing success, to "knock the fool" out of each other.

When Sooner guard Ralph Stevenson was leveled by a strong forearm to his face, he got even by swinging and kicking at his assailant. Sick and tired of all the street fighting, the refs threw Stephenson and two other players out of the game.

As the hostilities increased, Tennessee coach General Robert Neyland noticed that his center, Jim Rike, was involved in more than his share of fracases. So Neyland called for second string center Joe Little to replace Rike. The coach told Little, a senior and one of the cooler heads on the squad, to settle down his teammates and get their minds back on football.

Little had good intentions—until his first play. As he snapped the ball back for a punt, Little was lifted off the ground by an uppercut to his chin. Tossing aside his role as peacemaker, Little chased his attacker downfield and delivered an equally vicious blow. He then stood over the fallen Sooner and dared him to get up. The referee threw Little out of the game just 30 seconds after he had been sent into the fray to cool things down.

No one was safe from the brutal playing—not even the cheerleaders. When the Volunteers ran a sweep for a touchdown, they were so intense that they bowled over an unlucky Tennessee cheerleader and knocked her unconscious.

CIGAR BOWL

Dec. 30, 1912

What started out as a friendly post-season game between teams from the United States and Cuba erupted into a gridiron version of the Bay of Pigs fiasco. The Cigar Bowl, as it was unofficially called, left players, fans, and police smoking in anger.

The Florida Gators were invited to Havana to play the island nation's championship football team, the Cuban Athletic Club, in a holiday spectacle designed to foster relations between the neighboring countries. The contest almost severed relations.

The problem was that the referee did everything within his power to throw the game to the Cuban team—the same team he had once coached.

Twice during the first quarter, Gator touchdowns were called back by the ref after he slapped Florida with nonexistent penalties on the plays. In fact, whenever the Gators managed to run for a big chunk of yardage, the ref wiped out the gain with a convenient penalty.

Although Florida outplayed the Cubans, the game remained scoreless as coach G.E. Pyle steamed and stewed over the ref's cheating. Midway through the contest, the Gators stopped the Cubans on fourth down, but the offensive line dragged and pushed the runner to a first down. Coach Pyle protested vociferously and demanded that the ref call the required 15-yard penalty. The ref, acting more like a street market vendor than an official, decided to bargain with the incensed coach and suggested Pyle settle for just a 5-yard penalty.

Pyle refused to negotiate, so the ref gave him an ultimatum: Either take the 5 yards or nothing at all. The coach ended the showdown by ordering his stunned Gators to march off the field. In retaliation, the ref declared the game forfeited to the Cuban Athletic Club.

As the 1,500 fans in the stands booed the Florida team, police streamed onto the field. Since Cuban law mandated that a game could not be forfeited, Pyle was arrested, whisked to the police station, and eventually released to stand trial the next day.

Pyle, however, did not wait for his day in Cuban court. He and his team booked passage aboard the ship Olivette and fled Havana just an hour before the trial was slated to begin.

When the Gators fled, plans for another Cigar Bowl went up in smoke.

WORLD BOWL I

Dec. 5, 1974

It should have been called the Hunger Bowl.

The World Football League's first, last, and only championship game featured two starving teams so deeply in debt that the player rosters read like welfare rolls.

The Florida Blazers and the Birmingham Americans were well-matched—they were both the woebegones of football.

No player on either squad had received a regular paycheck for weeks, although Florida held the edge in experience because it had had a 14-week no-pay streak—which was nearly three times longer than Birmingham's.

Nevertheless, the Americans were the ones who went on strike just three days before the game. They walked off the practice field demanding five weeks of unpaid wages. A day later, they relented and went back to work; Birmingham owner Bill Putnam promised them they would receive championship rings if they won the World Bowl.

That was a tenuous promise, considering that the Americans owed the IRS $237,000 in back taxes and had already agreed to give the lion's share of the game's gate to the feds. Furthermore, the team's coffers were so sparse that coach Jack Gotta had to pay for his team's pre-game meal out of his own pocket.

In spite of Birmingham's woes, Florida was still the sentimental favorite to win the World Bowl because it had suffered even greater deprivation. The Blazer ownership had last paid its players and coaches nearly three months earlier, and mostly with rubber checks. Adding to their troubles was the fact that the managing general partner had sued the owner, and the owner sued the managing general partner. The financial picture was so bleak that coach Jack Pardee and his assistants took turns buying toilet paper for the team's clubhouse. The coaches also invited players to their homes for dinner to be sure the guys got a hot meal every now and then.

For the Blazers, trying to cash a personal check was harder than running back a kickoff for a touchdown. The worst moment for Pardee came when he had trouble paying for a purchase at a convenience store with *cash*. "The clerk looked at my $20 bill and made some remark about it possibly being counterfeit," said the beleaguered coach. Somehow the team endured.

Having been stiffed by management for months, the Blazers were looking for fair treatment on the field. But they were also robbed by the refs in the first quarter of the game. Florida running back Tommy Reamon appeared to have scored on a five-yard burst off tackle, but the referees ruled he had fumbled before reaching the end zone. (Instant replays revealed that Reamon had fumbled *after* he had scored. Snarled Blazer linebacker Bill Hobbs, "The WFL officiating is even worse than not getting paid!") The bad call seemed to dim the Blazers' fighting spirit; they trailed 15–0 at halftime.

Between halves, the WFL presented the league's Most Valuable Player Award. Three rookies tied for the $10,000 award and were to receive $3,333.33 each. (There was talk that the winners would have a choice of taking a WFL check in that amount or a WFL franchise.) Giving the three players checks would have spurred ridicule from the fans, so the league arranged for armed Wells Fargo guards to deliver cold cash to the winners right on the field.

In the second half, the Americans built up to a 22–0 lead and then held on for dear life to win 22–21 as a furious Blazer rally fell short— just like their cash flow.

Out of frustration, the Blazers started a fight on almost every one of the last few plays. After the gun sounded, Florida cornerback Billy Hayes stole the game ball and raced toward the Blazer dressing room. Birmingham tackle Paul Costa chased him, and several players from both teams pursued the two of them. It was a bizarre scene. Players who hadn't been paid for weeks were fighting over a football. Hayes managed to hold on to the ball.

The Americans soon discovered they should have been more concerned with holding on to something other than the ball. While the victors doused each other with champagne in their locker room, a process server walked in with a court order to seize their uniforms on behalf of a creditor.

Only in the World Bowl could the winners lose their shirts. And their pants, and their shoes, and their helmets.

CRUD DUDS

Some teams have proven to the world that there truly is no accounting for taste. How else can you explain why certain squads run around looking like they just escaped from a Barnum & Bailey sideshow? Their uniforms deserve to be placed on irrevocable waivers. For "The Most Awful Uniforms Ever Worn," The Football Hall of SHAME inducts the following:

GREEN BAY PACKERS

Sept. 1, 1937

For the new 1937 season, Green Bay coach Curly Lambeau purchased expensive, new green and gold uniforms because he wanted his champion Packers to look like winners.

But the first time the team wore them in a game, the jerseys made the Packers losers.

Lambeau introduced the new Packer uniforms when his team, the 1936 NFL champions, played against the College All-Stars at Chicago's Soldier Field in football's annual summer charity event.

Decked out in their new duds, the Green Bay players looked sharp. But by the end of the game, they were wilted, wrinkled, and limp. Not the jerseys—the players. The Packers looked like they had been run through the wash and hung out to dry. To their horror, they discovered that their nice new jerseys were made of synthetic material that did not breathe; the Packers were undergoing almost unbearable suffering in the hot, sticky night.

The new uniforms did more damage to Green Bay than did the All Stars' front line. Every few minutes a Packer staggered off the field, weak-kneed and sick. Some players dropped ten, fifteen, and even twenty pounds from water loss in their sauna-tized jerseys.

The collegians, wearing traditional, cooler uniforms, wore down the Packers, who simply couldn't handle the heat or humidity. In the third quarter, the weary pros managed to drive down to the All-Stars' 3-yard line. But the Packers were too sapped to punch the ball across the goal. They lost possession on downs, frittering away their only big scoring chance of the night. It was the first time in three years that they had failed to score once inside the 5-yard line.

The Packers lost the game 6–0. The team also lost their new jerseys; Coach Lambeau immediately packed them away—for good.

Although the players cursed the jerseys privately, they didn't blame the loss on the uniforms publicly. That's because they didn't want to anger the man responsible for the goof, their hot-tempered coach. In addition, the Packers thought the uniform issue would be perceived by fans as a weak excuse for getting beat up by a bunch of college boys.

In truth, the score should have read: Jerseys 6, Packers 0.

WORLD FOOTBALL LEAGUE

July, 1975

In a bizarre attempt to add color to the game, melon heads in the World Football League office approved uniforms that would have turned the teams into human fruit salads.

For the exhibition season, the league decided to experiment with color-coded pants aimed at helping spectators identify various player positions. (Apparently, the WFL didn't think highly of its fans' intelligence.)

In the experiment, different colored pants would designate the positions of the players: purple for offensive linemen, green for running backs, orange for wide receivers, blue for defensive linemen, red for linebackers, yellow for deep backs, and white with colored stars down the leg for quarterbacks.

When the fancy pants arrived for the Memphis Grizzlies, the players showed good taste—they refused to wear them.

Paul Warfield studied his orange trousers with the black vertical stripes for a long moment and said, "I've spent eleven years in professional football trying to build a serious image. I'm too far along in my career to begin playing Emmett Kelly."

Added teammate Jim Kiick, eyeing his greenies, "I'd look like a lime tree—or some kind of fruit."

Larry Csonka threw the offending garment onto the floor of the locker room and sneered, "Sure, and the coaches are going to wear shocking pink suits with high heels and those little lace caps they like so much. Heck, these pants are what the owners wear up in their air-conditioned suites when they watch the game. They figure it's only right that we dress as nicely as they do."

After the players informed the league they would not dress up like bananas, kumquats, and prunes, the league finally agreed to toss the uniforms.

If the WFL had wanted fruits, they should have set up a franchise in Key West.

Y.A. TITTLE

Cornerback · Louisiana State Tigers · Nov. 1, 1947

Y.A. Tittle would have been the hero of a crucial Southeastern Conference battle if his uniform had performed as well as he did.

In the second quarter of a key game against the visiting Mississippi Rebels, Tittle picked off a Charley Conerly pass intended for Barney Poole at the LSU 15-yard line. Before Y.A. could make tracks for the opposite end zone, Poole grabbed hold of the back of Tittle's belt. As Tittle struggled to get free, his belt broke.

His gold pants began a slow descent. But Y.A. took off anyway, holding the ball in his left hand and keeping his pants up with his right. To his joy, Tittle saw an open field ahead of him. To his horror, he realized his pants were slipping lower and lower.

Suddenly, a Rebel closed in on him from the left side, so Tittle switched the ball to his right hand. But when he went to grab his pants with the other hand, he was too late. His pants had fallen down! And so did he—at the LSU 38-yard-line.

"If my pants hadn't fallen, I'd have scored easily," recalled Tittle, who put this mortifying episode behind him to become a stellar NFL quarterback and Hall of Famer.

"It was really an embarrassing moment. There I was down to my jock strap out in front of 50,000 people. I kept asking my teammates to surround me, but they didn't help me a damn bit. They were all laughing so hard they couldn't do anything. Everybody was getting such a chuckle out of it except me."

The Tigers weren't laughing so hard when they realized that Tittle could have scored the winning touchdown if it hadn't been for those pants. LSU failed to score on that series and lost the game 20–18.

"I was running for the winning touchdown, or at least to a spot where we could have kicked the winning field goal," Tittle said. "But we lost and Ole Miss went to the Sugar Bowl instead of us. Losing my pants kept us out of the Sugar Bowl. Imagine, I got tackled by my own pants."

PITTSBURGH PIRATES

1934

It was criminal what Art Rooney did to his team. The owner of the Pittsburgh Pirates (which eventually changed its name to the Steelers) clad his players in striped jerseys that made them look like fugitives from a chain gang.

"The uniforms were pretty bad," recalled Armand Niccolai, a tackle and kicker who wore the prison garb. "But since we had to buy our own shoes, helmets, and pads, we were just thankful to have uniforms."

Once the season started, however, the Pirates would have been willing to play in their skivvies to avoid the razzing from their opponents. "The other teams really got on us a lot about our uniforms," said Niccolai. "They called us 'the chain gang' and 'jailbirds.'" The uniforms were so ridiculous that fans half expected to see the officials bring out a ball and chain for measurements.

Because they were forced to wear the most outlandish uniforms ever seen on a pro gridiron, the embarrassed Pirates can be pardoned for their lousy year—they finished the season with a dismal 2–10 record. The following year, the jailhouse jerseys were dumped. Said Niccolai, in a classic understatement, "Everybody was sure glad to see them go."

SAM McALLESTER

Fullback · Tennessee Volunteers · Nov. 24, 1904

In a game against Alabama, Sam McAllester showed up with an ingeniously sneaky accessory to his uniform. He wore a wide leather belt that had a leather loop sewn onto each side.

At first, the puzzled Alabama players couldn't figure out what the loops were for. Midway through the second quarter of a scoreless game, they found out.

After the Volunteers took possession of the ball at midfield, they ran the same play over and over. McAllester received the handoff, ran forward, and planted his foot on the back of one of the guards. Then his two backfield mates, the Caldwell brothers, each grabbed a loop of his belt and simply hurled him over the line. The play picked up at least 5 yards every time. By repeatedly catapulting McAllester, Tennessee drove down the field. They scored the game's only touchdown when he was thrown into the end zone.

Alabama had been thrown for a loop by McAllester's underhanded belt.

DENVER BRONCOS

1960–61

The Denver Broncos were the "laughing socks" of professional football. They wore vertically striped hose.

The hideous socks, which looked like they were stolen from a Ringling Brothers clown act, were so comical that several players wanted to play barefoot. Others collected money to give to management for new socks, but their offer was turned down.

The socks accentuated the disgusting uniforms that the Broncos donned during their first two years in the AFL. General manager Dean Griffing had bought the striped hose, along with ugly brown jerseys and gold pants, at a bargain price from the defunct Copper Bowl. Such a deal.

After enduring snickers and snide remarks from fans and opponents for two seasons, the Broncos were spared further humiliation when new head coach Jack Faulkner changed the team's colors to orange and blue. He also decided that the ridiculous looking socks had to go.

Faulkner, however, knowing this was cause for celebration, didn't just have the equipment man dispose of the hose. Instead, the coach held the Great Sock Barbeque, attended by thousands of fans, at the club's practice field. There, just before the opening of the season, the players trotted around the field, holding up their hose. And then, as the crowd applauded, the socks were tossed onto a huge bonfire. Nobody tried to hose them down.

SIDELINE SIDEWINDERS

Those who can, do. Those who can't, teach. Those who can't do either, coach. And sometimes they don't do that very well. The lucky ones can mishandle players, draw up a crummy game plan, call the wrong plays, and still win because they have the talented players. But even if they try to hide behind their win-loss record, their faults become glaring enough for all to see. For "The Most Disgraceful Coaches," The Football Hall of SHAME inducts the following:

WOODY HAYES

Coach • Ohio State Buckeyes • 1951–78

Woody Hayes always preached that football developed character, leadership, and sportsmanship. But he seldom showed any of those qualities on the sidelines.

Hayes threw outrageous on-the-field tantrums, screamed vile abuse at officials, and slugged anyone within reach—even his own players. This full-grown man attached so much importance to football that he acted like a child. He won 238 games, but lost respect because of his uncontrollable fits of rage.

For twenty-eight years, Ohio State shrugged off these embarrassments. But when Hayes punched Charlie Bauman of Clemson University in the closing moments of the 1979 Gator Bowl, the school tossed Hayes out on his ear.

With 1:58 left in the Buckeyes' 17–15 loss to Clemson, Bauman, a Tiger linebacker, intercepted an Ohio State pass and was knocked out of bounds at Hayes' feet. The gray-haired leader of young men was so upset by the turnover that he let loose with a roundhouse right to Bauman's chops. Hayes' fists were still flailing when his own athletes

overpowered him. While restraining Hayes, Ohio State player Ken Fritz
was socked in the face by the raging coach.

This was the last degrading incident in a pattern of revolting behavior
that stained the otherwise distinguished record of the hot-tempered
coach.

Woody threw his most famous tantrum in front of 104,016 fans during
a 10–7 loss to hated rival Michigan in 1971. He roared out onto the field
claiming a Wolverine interception should have been ruled pass interference. Hayes squared off for a fight with a sideline official, but never
touched him. Instead, he hurled obscenities at all the refs. It cost him a
15-yard penalty for unsportsmanlike conduct. After a platoon of assistant
coaches dragged him back to the sidelines, Hayes grabbed the downs
marker out of the hands of an official and tried to break it. Then he shot
it, javelin style, onto the field. Next, the rampaging madman headed for
the first down marker, ripped off the bright orange plastic encasement,
tore it to shreds, and flung the remnants onto the field.

Hayes showed similar respect for the media. After losing 17–0 to the
University of Southern California in the 1959 Rose Bowl, Hayes shoved a
sportswriter against a locker room wall. Later, he swung at another
reporter and luckily missed.

Just before kickoff at the 1973 Rose Bowl game, Hayes became
enraged at *Los Angeles Times* photographer Art Rogers, who was snapping close-ups of him as he huddled with his assistants. Without warning, Hayes charged at Rogers, shoving the camera into his face and
bowling him over. "That ought to take care of you, you son of a bitch!"
Hayes yelled. The photographer suffered from double vision and swollen
eyes for several weeks.

With millions of TV viewers watching in 1977, Woody slammed down
his field phone and charged at ABC television cameraman Mike Fried-

man after a Buckeye fumble during a 14–6 defeat to Michigan. Viewers saw their TV picture swing wildly out of control when Hayes aimed a punch at the cameraman's midsection. For the attack, the Big Ten Conference put Hayes on a one-year probation. He showed his regret by saying, "I make no apologies."

Hayes was often just as brutal to his own players as he was to his enemies. Once, when freshman fullback Pete Johnson (who later became an NFL star) had missed several blocks during a practice scrimmage, Hayes shouted, "Fullback, you're the biggest goddamned jackass I've ever seen! Block, you dumb son of a bitch!" He marched up to Johnson and swatted him hard on the shoulder pads. When Johnson again moved toward the wrong hole on the next play, Hayes erupted into a purple-faced frenzy. Biting down hard on the heel of his own hand, Hayes whirled around in a fury, grabbed his own T-shirt at the neck, and tore it to shreds.

During practice, Hayes always wore a black Ohio State baseball cap and a flaming red T-shirt. He watched with arms folded, jaw jutting, and paunch protruding. Occasionally, before a practice, he used a razor blade to slice the threads of his cap so that when he went berserk over some foul-up the cap tore easily, and more menacingly.

Woody had no trouble enlisting jeers and boos from fans when the Buckeyes played on the road. In game after game, he whipped his cap off, flung it to the ground, and stomped on it. He also did the same thing with his watch or glasses (although, somehow, he usually managed to miss them with his stomps).

He kicked at everything from chairs to equipment. But he controlled his toe after he kicked a sideline marker that he thought was made of rubber. It turned out to be made of concrete.

RICHARD NIXON

President • United States of America • 1969–74

As a self-appointed assistant coach, President Richard Nixon was as successful as his Watergate defense.

Without ever being asked, Nixon suggested plays to pro coaches who, out of some patriotic duty, actually followed his advice. What a shame. The plays never worked.

Nixon fancied himself as a football expert, even though his only football experience was that of an enthusiastic bench warmer for Whittier College. Nevertheless, when he was vice-president, he began offering plays to his favorite team, the Washington Redskins.

He often sat in a special box with team owner George Marshall and gave his recommendations. Once, during a 1958 game, Nixon suggested that the Redskins' aging defensive end Gene Brito play offense so he could catch a pass. Moments after Marshall picked up the phone and relayed the message to the bench, Brito lined up with the offense. Sure enough, a pass was thrown right to Brito, but he forgot to look for it. The ball hit him squarely in the back.

Undeterred, Nixon continued to give the Redskin coaches advice— bad advice. Before the 1971 divisional play-off clash between Washington and the San Francisco 49ers, the President telephoned Redskin coach George Allen and said, "I'd like to see you run a flanker reverse with Roy Jefferson."

Late in the second quarter of the game, Washington was faced with second down and 6 yards to go on the San Francisco 8-yard line. Allen called for Nixon's play; Jefferson ran a flanker reverse. The result: a 13-yard loss. The Redskins went on to lose 24–20.

Once Washington was eliminated from the play-offs, Nixon switched allegiances to the Miami Dolphins, who were gearing up for the Dallas Cowboys in Super Bowl VI. Because the Dolphins were the underdogs, Nixon felt the team needed his help. So, while he put the Vietnam War on hold, he phoned Dolphins coach Don Shula at 1 A.M., ten days before the big game. "I thought it was some idiot calling at that late hour," recalled Shula.

Nixon told Shula the way to beat Dallas was to send Miami's star wide receiver Paul Warfield on some simple down-and-in pass patterns. Four times in the Super Bowl, the Dolphins tried Nixon's play. And four times the Cowboys foiled it, including once for an interception. Miami was creamed 24–3.

Calling Nixon "the assistant coach of the Miami Dolphins," the Dallas Bonehead Club presented the President with its coveted Bonehead Trophy "for insuring a Dallas victory by sending some of his plays to Coach Shula."

The next year, the Dolphins won the Super Bowl. After thanking half the world, Shula added, "I also want to thank the President for offering *not* to send in any more plays."

GEORGE ALLEN

Coach · Los Angeles Rams–Washington Redskins · 1966–78

No winning coach was a bigger loser in the clubhouse than George Allen.

Players despised him and owners fired him. They rejected his penchant for spartan practices, his obsession with neatness, and his maniacal insistence on victory.

To Allen, winning was more important than life itself. To prove it, he tried to drum into his players' heads his favorite motto, "Losing is like dying." He was so fanatical that he would do anything to win—including trading draft choices he didn't own and filing false injury reports with the NFL office.

Allen was once accused of spying on an enemy team by having a mother push a baby carriage past the opponent's practice field. According to the accusations, the mother was not the spy; Allen had hired a midget to sit in the carriage and take notes. When reporters questioned him about the alleged incident, Allen laughed.

Victory meant more to him than his own flesh and blood. Coaching the Redskins in a game against the Philadelphia Eagles in 1973, Allen denied the identity of his son Bruce rather than risk a penalty. Bruce, a teenager at the time, was wearing a credential that restricted him to the

Redskin bench. But during the game, Bruce roamed far downfield on the sideline to harass the Eagle quarterback. Finally, the referee stopped play, grabbed Bruce, and brought him to Allen. "Is this a member of your staff?" the ref asked the coach. Allen, figuring he faced a possible 15-yard bench misconduct penalty, knew exactly what to say: "I've no idea. He must be one of those people the Eagles gave us as ballboys."

Under his warped philosophy, Allen freely encouraged his players to fight with opponents during games—and even with each other during practice. After a free-for-all between the St. Louis Cardinals and his Redskins, Allen told the press, "I loved the fight. If we didn't go out there and fight, I'd be worried. The guys who sit on the bench are losers." As coach of the Rams in 1966, Allen fostered an intra-clubhouse bout—"just to get 'em going, just to get 'em all together."

Although Allen never had a losing season in his 12-year NFL career as head coach, he holds the record for the earliest dismissal in league history. In his second tour of duty with the Rams, he was fired by owner Carroll Rosenbloom in August 1978 after just two exhibition games.

Part of the reason Allen was fired was a player revolt after Allen instituted a grueling, prolonged schedule of two-a-days. Practicing at a hot, smog-choked camp in the heart of the Los Angeles basin, Rams players were forced to earn each drink. Team doctors begged Allen to include water breaks after seven dehydrated players collapsed on a single July afternoon. "George just rams the accelerator down to the floor like Mario Andretti," one player complained to the *Los Angeles Times*. "If the car lasts, it lasts; if not, he just throws it away and gets a new car."

If it wasn't his Simon Legree approach to football, it was his compulsion for tidiness that bugged everyone on the team. Allen actually gave a reward to the player with the neatest notebook. "George was almost obsessive about things like a wastebasket with one scrap of paper in it or a blackboard that was anything but absolutely clean," said Rosenbloom.

Allen was proud of his fixation, and told reporters, "I don't want to see one [empty] Gatorade cup on the field. The goal posts must be padded properly and the field has to be watered just enough. When you're through with the blackboard it must be erased clean. The light bulbs in the meeting room must be covered and there must be no unnecessary noise anytime, anyplace."

The Rams management decided there would be no more George Allen rules anytime, anyplace.

FRANK KUSH

Coach ▪ Arizona State Sun Devils ▪ 1958–79

Frank Kush represented all that is shameful about the win-at-all-costs mentality.

Kush believed players performed best when they were afraid, so he coached using fear, punishment, and pain. In practice, he struck players with boards, ropes, tree branches, and a metal rod. He insulted and humiliated players in front of teammates. He also forced them to play while injured, and put them through torturous conditioning drills until they collapsed.

A self-styled tough guy, Kush was notorious for driving his players beyond their physical and emotional limits, which explains why his pre-season practice in the Tonto National Forest was known as Kush's Koncentration Kamp. He slapped helmets, kicked butts, yanked face masks, and doled out punishment laps up a 500-foot hillock that players called Mount Kush.

But the worst punishment of all was the Hamburger Drill. It ruined many young players, such as former linebacker Darby Jones. "During practice scrimmage, I jumped offside and Kush ran over to me with such an angry look I thought he was going to hit me, so I stepped back and raised my hands," Jones recalled. "He looked at me and said, 'Okay, let's see how you do in the Hamburger Drill.'

"Kush had the entire defensive team circle around me and ordered me to get in the middle in a three-point stance. Then when he blew his whistle, they came at me one at a time while I tried to block them. After about ten times, I was beaten to the ground, but Kush was still so angry he kept blowing his whistle. By now I was getting hit and speared even before I could get up.

"One of the players finally felt sorry for me and just laid on top of me. But Kush got real mad at him and put him in the Hamburger Drill while the trainer dragged me away. I was all beat up and bleeding. I decided if all college football was like Frank Kush's football, I didn't want any part of it."

Other players who failed to make the grade were further humiliated by Kush. He made them hitchhike back to campus fifty miles away. Those who stayed paid—in pain. To punish a receiver who dropped a pass in practice, Kush made him repeatedly jump up for high passes so the defensive backs could cut his legs out from under him. When a quarterback didn't drop back quickly enough, Kush took away the whole offensive line except for the center and made the quarterback run the plays virtually alone. Naturally, the defense repeatedly rushed in and clobbered him.

Few people complained about Kush's excesses and heavy-handed tactics because he produced winning teams. In his 21½ years at Arizona State, Kush compiled a 176–54–1 record.

But his deplorable coaching style was exposed to public scrutiny in 1979 when former player Kevin Rutledge sued him. Rutledge, a punter, claimed that he had kicked poorly in a 1978 game when Kush grabbed him, shook his helmet from side to side, and unloaded a punch under Rutledge's face mask that caught the player in the mouth. Although Rutledge lost the suit, Kush was fired over accusations that he tried to cover up the slugging incident.

During the trial, in which Kush was called a "sadistic animal," the coach denied ever punching or kicking players. He did admit, however, striking players with lengths of rope in "what I would call a fatherly affectionate tap." (Sure, and Marvelous Marvin Hagler's knockout punch was a friendly pat.) Kush also testified that his disciplinary methods helped "eliminate the fear factor." Most often, they did just the opposite.

RAH, RAH, RAH, HISS BOO BAH!

*There are some things the world could do just fine without. War ...
famine ... pestilence ... four-legged team mascots. Who needs
them? Fans go to the stadium to watch the game; if they want
animals, let the spectators go to the zoo. That's where most of the
mascots belong anyway. Some of their antics on the sidelines are so
beastly even the ASPCA would want to see the perpetrators put
away. For "The Most Pathetic Performances by Mascots," The Football Hall of SHAME inducts the following:*

SEAL

Mascot • University of Virginia • 1947–53

Seal was a lazy, drunken mutt. Only one thing inspired him at games.
During halftime, he would pee on the goal posts of the opposing team.

A legend in his own time, the black and white dog of undetermined
ancestry had a leg up on all other mascots in dampening the spirits of
the enemy. His most dubious antic came in Philadelphia, when Virginia
played the University of Pennsylvania in 1949.

Seconds before the halftime gun sounded, Seal headed for the Penn
goal posts. The Penn cheerleaders were prepared, however, and they
formed a line, blocking the dog's path. Seal pondered this dilemma for a
moment. Then he made a beeline for the abandoned cheerleader bench
and proceeded to pee on their megaphones.

Back on campus between gigs, Seal concentrated on his favorite
pastime—lapping up beer. "It was a common sight to see this slow,
bowlegged dog stagger home at night from some frat party," recalled

John Herring, head of the school's student activity center. "All that beer may have had something to do with his tendency to irrigate on the opposing team's things."

Seal paid for his boozing with his life. The mutt died in 1953 from what a school official termed "overindulgence." More than 2,000 mourners attended his funeral. An antique black hearse bore his flower-draped casket and led a long processional made more solemn by the muffled roll of drums beating out the slow, somber "Death March." Behind the hearse walked students, townspeople, and school administrators. Nasty, a mongrel who considered himself the heir apparent to Seal's throne, marched with a black mourning band around one leg.

At the grave site, Dr. Charles Frankel, the team physician, delivered the eulogy, which said in part, "I can see Seal now leading the parade in a celestial stadium with golden hydrants and guilded megaphones at his disposal, megaphones such as the one at the University of Pennsylvania where Seal passed his acid test with flying colors."

BEVO

Mascot ▪ Texas Longhorns ▪ 1916–present

As a mascot for the University of Texas, Bevo has been nothing but a lot of bull.

Actually, there have been twelve bovines that have carried the sacred name Bevo. The last two, Bevo XI and Bevo XII, have dutifully performed their jobs as the school's official Longhorn. But the actions of the previous ten have given Texas fans plenty to beef about.

Being a lazy cuss, Bevo I (1916–20) didn't serve too well as the school's mascot. In 1920, however, he did serve as a steak dinner at a large football banquet.

Next came the imposter, Bevo II (1932). He couldn't fool Texas fans, who quickly spotted him for what he really was—a Hereford masquerading as a Longhorn. Because of his ancestry, he was retired after one year. He did experience one moment of ignobility. He charged after a Southern Methodist University cheerleader, who deftly sidestepped him and then bonked him over the head with a megaphone.

Bevo III (1945–48) didn't just bite the hand that fed him—he tried to crush it in a one-bull stampede. One day he broke loose and terrorized the campus until he was captured and hauled away for good.

Bevo IV (1949) was a red, ornery, 1,700-pound beast. In his debut, he battered a parked car before his 11 handlers brought him under control. But after he leaped over an eight-foot fence, they realized he was just too much steer for them to handle.

The meanest Texas mascot of all was Bevo V (1950–54). Fans often drove to the ranch where he was kept during the week just to see how he was doing. On several occasions, they returned to campus with cuts and bruises, or with ripped and bloodied clothes. He was so strong he kicked down half a side of a barn. In the lowlight of his career, he broke loose at a football game and scattered the panic-stricken Baylor University marching band.

Bevo VI (1955–56) wasn't tough enough to be the school's mascot. The shouting and noise of football games scared him. Handlers often had to drag him out. Once he tried to hightail it out of the stadium and ran right over the Rice University bench.

Nothing that exciting ever happened to Bevo VII (1957–65) and Bevo VIII (1965–66). They were rather dull and boring, so eventually they were turned out to pasture. Bevo IX (1966–76) pretty much followed in their hoofprints, except for one bizarre quirk. He had this thing about women—he hated them. He'd just as soon stomp on them as look at them.

None of the Bevos were quite as shameful as Bevo X (1976–81). He didn't exactly create the illusion of invincibility and fierceness. Since he couldn't cope with the excitement of each game, he was tranquilized slightly. Then all he did was stand around or lay down, causing some disgusted fans to hurl the ultimate insult. They called him Bevo the *Cow*. It didn't help his image any when Texas running star Earl Campbell crashed into him in the end zone during a game. Campbell got up quickly after the collision. But Bevo X, who had been lying down, stayed down.

SOONER SCHOONER

Mascot ▪ Oklahoma Sooners ▪ Jan. 1, 1985

The Oklahoma Sooners' pep squad brought their mascot onto the field sooner than they should—which ended up costing their team 3 points.

Early in the fourth quarter of the 1985 Orange Bowl, Oklahoma's Tim Lashar kicked a 22-yard field goal to give the Sooners an apparent 17–14 lead over the Washington Huskies. But a flag had been thrown on the play. Oklahoma was caught in an illegal formation and penalized 5 yards, which negated the boot.

Oklahoma senior Rex Harris, however, didn't see the flag. Harris was the driver of the Sooner Schooner, the midget-sized covered wagon hauled by two small white ponies that gallop onto the field after every Oklahoma score. The Ruf-Neks, a pep group in charge of the Schooner, directed Harris to take the Schooner onto the field.

When he did, Harris didn't hear the cheers he expected. All he heard was the angry voices of the referees, who ordered the Schooner off the

field. "As soon as we got on the field, the ref started yelling, 'Fifteen yard penalty!' I had no idea what was going on," Harris recalled. He and the team quickly found out.

The Sooner Schooner's premature excursion prompted a 15-yard unsportsmanlike conduct penalty against Oklahoma. Added to the Sooners' 5-yard illegal procedure penalty, the new penalty meant kicker Tim Lashar had to try a field goal from 20 yards further away. His 42-yard attempt was blocked. The momentum swung toward Washington, which went on to claim a 28–17 victory.

The following year, Oklahoma returned for the 1986 Orange Bowl clash against Penn State. Not wanting to take any more chances, officials docked the Schooner and kept it off the turf. It was bound to happen Sooner or later.

GUMBO

Mascot • New Orleans Saints • 1967–present

For its capers, Gumbo the mascot has always belonged in the doghouse.

Back in 1967, the New Orleans Restaurant Association gave the Saints a St. Bernard puppy that was named after the city's most famous concoction. It was Gumbo's job to rally the fans and players from the sidelines. But the team's first mascot quickly sniffed the odor of a terrible team and awaited his chance to escape. After witnessing four straight losing seasons, he ran away.

He was replaced by Gumbo II, a female that once tried to help the Saints by chasing Pittsburgh Steeler quarterback Terry Bradshaw. He was scrambling for a touchdown when Gumbo II broke loose and tried to tackle him (none of the Saints could do it). Barking and snarling, Gumbo II tore after Bradshaw, who ran into the end zone for a TD and then sprinted even faster to the safety of the Pittsburgh bench.

But when her spirit failed to inspire the Saints, Gumbo II turned to drink for solace. "She always had to have a couple of beers to prep for the game because she knew what was coming up and she hated it so much," said her trainer and owner Larry Dale. "Before every game, she went to the press box and begged a beer or two. I guess the only way she could stand to watch the Saints was to get juiced up."

Eventually, even the booze couldn't help her cope with watching the Saints. By the halftime of each game, she went from the sidelines to the locked gate leading to the clubhouse and whined, barked, and scratched to be let off the field. She soon died of a stomach ailment. Apparently, said Dale, "the Saints had made her sick to death."

Gumbo III knew right from the start that she wanted no part of the Saints. In her debut, she literally had to be dragged out onto the field. Frightened by the crowd noise, she squatted and christened the Superdome carpet. Then she curled up in a big lump and went to sleep. She repeated this performance at most every game.

Gumbo IV topped her predecessor. "Every time we brought her onto the field, she'd always take a crap," said Dale. "She did in the Superdome what the Saints did on the field."

MAUDINE ORMSBY

Homecoming Queen • Ohio State • Nov. 12, 1926

Maudine Ormsby was the ugliest homecoming queen ever elected.

She had a long, straight nose with wide nostrils, big ears that she could wiggle, teeth the size of piano keys, broad but bony hips, and widely bowed ribs. And was she fat! She stood only five feet tall and had a girth to match. She weighed half a ton.

Maudine, you see, was a cow. The Ohio State student body elected a pure-bred, prize-winning Holstein their 1926 homecoming queen.

When it was time for the school to choose a queen, the fraternities and sororities nominated their own candidates. But the independent students felt they had been shunned, so they decided to put up their own candidate. They picked Maudine. She sure wasn't pretty, but she did have a nice disposition and a helluva set of jugs. She immediately gained the support of the College of Agriculture.

Although the university enrollment totaled only 9,000 back then, more than 13,000 ballots were cast—the majority for Maudine. (She beat out such write-in contenders as evangelist Aimee McPherson, Queen Mary, Helen of Troy, and Sophie Tucker.)

Some of her legitimate two-legged opponents protested the rigged election, but the homecoming committee decided to milk the prank for all it was worth, and allowed Maudine to wear her crown.

Maudine's chaperones wouldn't permit her to appear in all the homecoming festivities because, after all, she was only four years old. However, for the Ohio State homecoming parade, she did ride majestically in a horse-drawn float.

Unfortunately, Maudine failed to inspire the football team. It lost to Michigan—to the udder disappointment of Ohio State fans.

PENALTY PANDEMONIUM

Football is like a great literary work—Crime and Punishment. With the way some players try to get away with murder during a game, you'd swear they lettered at Attica. But, like chronic felons, they usually get caught red-handed. Referees have thrown enough flags at these offenders to cover an entire football field. For "The Most Nefarious Infractions Ever Committed," The Football Hall of SHAME inducts the following:

WILLIAM "THE REFRIGERATOR" PERRY

Defensive Tackle–Fullback • Chicago Bears • Nov. 17, 1985

William Perry—Chicago's lovable, snaggle-toothed, 308-pound Teddy Bear—became the toast of America in his rookie year.

A defensive tackle who occasionally moonlighted as a part-time fullback, Perry was big (in every sense of the word) news. His presence in the backfield as a runner, receiver, and blocker earned him status as a national celebrity. It also earned him induction into The Football Hall of SHAME—for committing the most outrageous illegal-use-of-hands penalty in pro football history.

In the third quarter of a 44–0 blowout over the Dallas Cowboys, the Bears had a third-and-goal from the Dallas 2-yard line when Perry was inserted in the Chicago backfield to block for running back Walter Payton. When Payton received the handoff, the Fridge buried the first Dallas defender who was in his way. Other Cowboys had stacked Payton up at the line of scrimmage, however, so Perry took matters into his own massive hands. He picked up Payton like a picnic basket and tried to carry him into the end zone.

Perry should have known better—it's against the rules to aid a runner like that. He was flagged for illegal use of hands, a 10-yard infraction.

The penalty pushed the Bears back to the 1-yard line; they eventually settled for a field goal.

After the game, a teammate asked Perry, "What were you trying to do?"

"Trying to pick up the guy who was on Walter—and Walter, too," said the Fridge. "It was instinct. I just wanted to help my teammate. I didn't know you weren't allowed to do that." Ignorance of the law was no excuse. But in Perry's case, that's the way the rookie rumbled.

Although Payton hardly needed Perry's help—after all, Payton is the NFL's all-time leading rusher—he said he "appreciated" Perry's effort, and added, "I'm just glad William didn't fall on me."

If Payton had crossed the goal line on the play, he would have been the first player in history to score a touchdown with a refrigerator on his back.

CLEVELAND BROWNS VS. CHICAGO BEARS

Nov. 25, 1951

"Over and over you would hear the man say:
It's being called back—there's a flag on the play."
—*Cleveland Plain Dealer*

There were so many violations during a bloody battle between the Browns and the Bears that it looked like the Geneva Convention would have to be rewritten. It was a game that should have been officiated by a United Nations peacekeeping force rather than football referees.

The refs threw their flags an average of once every 96 seconds in the most penalty-marred game in NFL history. The officials stepped off an incredible 374 yards on 37 infractions. Cleveland was caught 21 times for a record total of 209 yards, while Chicago was nailed 16 times for 165 yards.

Street gangs armed with knives and chains have fought more cleanly than the Browns and Bears did. The teams played as if the rules—along with some bones—were made to be broken. They committed just about every infraction in the book, from unnecessary roughness (such as creaming the punter) to use of illegal equipment (Cleveland guard Bill Willis wore an outlawed knee brace). It was a savage game where slugging and holding took the place of blocking and tackling.

"This was the roughest game I ever saw," said one official. "We had to call them [penalties]. There was nothing else we could do. Why, there could have been a regular war out there."

What did he mean "could have been"? It *was* a war.

There was plenty of bad blood between the teams, and most of it was spilled on the field. The only combatants who quit punching, kicking, and cheating were the ones ejected from the game or carted off on stretchers. Early in the second quarter, for example, Cleveland punter Horace Gillom was leveled by a vicious, unnecessary hit by Wayne Hansen, who subsequently received a 15-yard penalty. But Gillom didn't want justice; he wanted revenge. Late in the game, he punched out Hansen—and was promptly given the old heave-ho by the officials.

During one offensive series for the Bears, Cleveland was penalized 3 straight times for personal fouls. The 15-yard infractions proved to be the Bears' best offensive weapon as the refs moved the ball from the Chicago 46-yard line to the Browns' 9-yard line. Two of those penalties nullified 2 interceptions, one a spectacular 94-yard return by Don Shula.

"As soon as I reached the end zone," Shula said, "I turned around to see if they were calling it back." Sure enough, they were. Browns' halfback Dopey Phelps verbally lashed out at the official and was banished from the field.

In the third quarter, a Cleveland kickoff turned into a human demolition derby as the Bears tried to bash the Browns out of commission. The refs called 2 penalties against Chicago—a personal foul and an unsportsmanlike conduct infraction. As a result, Cleveland kicked off from the Bears' 30-yard line. (The Browns tried an onside kick that Chicago recovered on its own 8-yard line.)

So many plays were called back in the game (won by Cleveland 42–21) that the players felt like golden retrievers in training. Their ears rang from the shrillness of the refs' whistles, and their eyes blurred from the flurry of thrown flags.

Late in the third quarter, Bears coach George Halas couldn't stand it any more. He charged onto the field to protest yet another penalty. That's when Browns captain Tony Adamle decided to assert himself. He walked up behind Halas, politely tapped him on the shoulder and said, "Would you please get the hell outta here?"

STETSON UNIVERSITY HATTERS

Nov. 12, 1947

When the Stetson Hatters blew their tops at the officials, the team triggered one of the longest continuous series of penalties ever called.

In a game against the Erskine College Flying Fleet in Due West, South

Carolina, Erskine returned the second half kickoff to its own 30-yard line. On the play, Stetson was called for clipping, and the refs advanced the ball to the Flying Fleet's 45-yard line.

The Hatters ranted and raved. Captain Tom Ewing, pointing to an injured comrade, argued vociferously that it was an Erskine player who had committed the dirty deed. When the rest of the incensed Stetson players joined in the protest, the peeved referee called another penalty against them, this time for unsportsmanlike conduct.

The official picked up the ball imperiously and moved it 15 more yards, to the Stetson 40-yard line. By now, Ewing and teammate Grant Wilbank were throwing a conniption fit. Pouring out vials of wrath, they pushed and shoved the refs. For their crime, the two were banished from the game—and the Hatters were assessed their third straight 15-yard penalty. Because of the Hatters' blaze of temper, the ball had gone from the Erskine 30-yard line to the Stetson 25-yard line without a single play being run.

The Hatters finally cooled down enough for the Flying Fleet to run a play from scrimmage. It lost a yard. But before the Stetson players could exult, the refs once again slapped them with a major penalty—for unnecessary roughness—and the ball was placed on their 11-yard line.

On the next play, the Flying Fleet scored a touchdown. Even though the record books will show a 70-yard scoring drive, Erskine's net offense was only 10 yards. The other 60 yards came courtesy of the mad Hatters.

JOHN MADDEN

Coach • Oakland Raiders • Nov. 2, 1975

John Madden, the purple-faced, arm-flailing coach whose sideline tantrums made referees wish they were temporarily deaf, was tagged with one of pro football's rarest penalties because he was dumb enough to tell the truth.

During the heat of battle, an irate coach will often berate an official until the zebra gives him the opportunity to back off and avoid a 15-yard unsportsmanlike-conduct penalty. It's an infraction very seldom called against NFL coaches. But then, not all coaches are like John Madden. His big mouth and honesty cost him the only penalty of his remarkable ten-year head-coaching career.

It happened during a game between his Oakland Raiders and the Denver Broncos, won by the visiting Raiders 42–17. Denver ball carrier

Floyd Little had run out of bounds at midfield before he was flipped head over heels by Oakland cornerback Jack Tatum. Because no player is supposed to tackle a runner once he crosses the sideline, line judge Jack Fette immediately threw his flag and called a 15-yard penalty against Tatum for unnecessary roughness. That sent Madden into a rage.

"I was walking back to my position when Madden shouted to me, 'You're a blind bastard!' " Fette recalled. "I turned around and asked him, 'What did you say?' I tried to give him a chance to get off the hook. We refs do this with all the coaches, and almost always they back down by turning away or mumbling that they were talking to one of their players.

"So I faced Madden and said, 'Who did you call a blind bastard?' Old John chose not to get out of this confrontation and snapped back, 'You, that's who! You look like the only blind bastard to me!' I figured, what the hell? If he wants another 15 yards, let's give it to him. So I threw my flag in the air and told him, 'Well, let's go another 15 yards then!' "

Referee Norm Schachter stepped off 30 yards, 15 for unnecessary roughness on Tatum and 15 for unsportsmanlike conduct on Madden. The ball went from the 50-yard line to the Oakland 20.

Madden then laced into Schachter, demanding, "What was my penalty for?"

"You called Jack a blind bastard—not once, but twice," Schachter replied.

"Hell, he asked me what I had said," Madden retorted in a rising voice. "I repeated it. What the hell did he ask me to repeat it for if he didn't want me to say it?"

ANDY CVERCKO

Guard • Dallas Cowboys • Sept. 23, 1962

Andy Cvercko committed the costliest infraction in NFL history.

Because of the resulting penalty, the Cowboys turned a dramatic 99-yard touchdown pass into a shocking safety against themselves.

Of all the times and of all the places to be caught, Cvercko picked the absolute worst moment. In a home game against the Pittsburgh Steelers, Dallas was losing 21–14 in the third quarter and had possession on its own 1-yard line. Cowboy quarterback Eddie LeBaron faded into the end zone and threw a deep pass to wide receiver Frank Clarke, who caught the ball on the 45-yard line and scampered untouched the rest of the way for an apparent 99-yard TD pass.

But the hometown fans' cheers turned to tears when they saw a flag thrown in the Dallas end zone. Cvercko had been caught holding Pittsburgh defensive lineman Big Daddy Lipscomb. The play was called back. Then, to the stunned amazement of the spectators, Cowboys, and even the Steelers, referee Emil Heintz signaled a safety for Pittsburgh.

Unknown to almost everyone except Heintz, there was a specific rule to cover Cvercko's heinous crime. Rule 9, Section 5, Article 2 stated: "It is a safety when the offense commits a foul and spot of enforcement is behind their goal line." Instead of climbing to a 21–21 tie, the Cowboys now trailed 23–14.

"I never heard of the rule," admitted Steeler coach Buddy Parker. "But it was a good time to find out."

Dallas coach Tom Landry was also unaware of the obscure rule. He rushed out onto the field in a rage and engaged in a heated argument with Heintz. The coach lost his temper, his voice—and some of his hair.

Meanwhile, the 19,478 fans in the Cotton Bowl began howling and booing in protest. After the free kick following the safety, Pittsburgh could not get a play off because of all the noise from the hooting crowd. In exasperation, Steeler quarterback Bobby Layne pulled his team to the sideline, where they stood for about 3 minutes until the fans calmed down.

Cvercko's penalty and the safety it caused were especially painful to the Cowboys. They lost the game 30–28 by that 2-point margin.

NORTHWESTERN WILDCATS

Nov. 8, 1947

Northwestern committed the most shameful series of penalties in collegiate history to turn sure victory into bitter defeat—after time had expired.

The Wildcats were hanging on to a slim 6–0 lead over the Ohio State Buckeyes. With time for only one more play, the Buckeyes tried a last-gasp pass from Northwestern's 12-yard line. But as the final gun sounded, defender Fatso Day intercepted the pass to secure the Wildcat win. Or so it seemed.

The officials had thrown a flag after noticing that Northwestern had 12 men on the field. The chagrined team was penalized 5 yards. More important, Ohio State was given one more chance to score—this time from the 7-yard line. But Buckeye back Rod Swinehart was stopped at the 3-yard line. The Wildcats jumped up and down in celebration. *Now* they could claim victory. Or so it seemed.

Incredibly, the officials called Northwestern offside, granting Ohio State yet another shot at winning even though the clock had expired. This time, the Buckeyes took advantage of the back-to-back Wildcat blunders and scored the tying touchdown on a pass from Pandel Savic to Jimmy Clark.

Now the best Northwestern could hope for was to block the kick and settle for a 6–6 deadlock. Sure enough, Emil Moldea's conversion attempt was batted down and the Wildcats breathed a sigh of relief. At least they could walk away with a tie. Or so it seemed.

Unbelievably, the refs caught Northwestern offside again! Given a reprieve, Moldea kicked the extra point straight and true. The Wildcats trudged off the field knowing they had penalized themselves right into a shocking 7–6 defeat.

STRAINING CAMPS

For some teams, pre-season practice is run by a hard-boiled task-master who makes Marine boot camp seem like a sleep-away summer camp. The workouts are so torturous and strenuous that the term sudden death takes on an ominous, new meaning. Players are forced to scrimmage both ways—dog-tired and dead-tired. For "The Cruelest Training Camps Ever Run," The Football Hall of SHAME inducts the following:

HOUSTON OILERS

1960–63

Survival at the first few Houston Oiler training camps didn't mean making the cut. It meant outlasting dive-bombing mosquitoes, Texas-sized cockroaches, sweatboxlike heat, health-wrecking conditions, and stomach-churning food.

The prisoners in Sing Sing lived a country club existence compared to the Oilers. Only at Houston's early training camps did players profusely thank "The Turk," football's bearer of bad news, for informing them that they had been released; back then, being cut was like getting sprung from the penitentiary.

At the Oilers' first camp in 1960, at Houston's Buff Stadium, the keenest competition centered on a blood feud between the players and the insects. Players became experts at warding off the blitz of twin-engine mosquitoes. You could tell which players the team valued highly by the number of cans of insect repellent the club gave them. Cockroaches homesteaded the lockers, turning them into crowded bug tenements with little room for football gear.

The locker room looked like a dungeon scene out of Hugo's *Les Miserables*. It was a stifling, smelly cesspool. Whenever it rained, the floor flooded, and shoes floated aimlessly across the room. To help players identify their wayward gear, the trainer put numbers on all the shoes.

If the lack of air conditioning in the suffocating, hot room didn't make a player swoon, the stench usually did. To thwart fainting on the field, the jerseys were sprayed with ammonia. But the disgusting combination of insect repellent, sweat, and ammonia in the locker room after practice could bring even the most hardened veteran to his knees.

When the team moved its training camp the following year to a deserted section of Ellington Air Force Base in Pasadena, Texas, not a single person complained—at first. Unfortunately, the place didn't have a football field. What it did have was ground more lethal than a mine field. It was strewn with enough broken beer bottles, crushed cans, and shrapnel to slice the entire team to shreds.

Even if the players made it through a day of practice unscathed, they still had to contend with a far more dangerous hazard—the cook. The Oilers had retained the services of the base cook, a lifer who wasted nothing. He cooked anything, even things starving vultures would have rejected. But when he tried to serve the team a dinner of barbecued liver, the players—and their stomachs—revolted.

In 1963, the players actually looked forward to training camp because it was moved to Colorado Springs, known for its cool, dry summers. When the Oilers arrived, though, it wasn't very cool—but it sure was dry. In fact, the area was suffering its worst drought and water shortage in thirty-six years.

With pure water at a premium, the practice field was irrigated with sewer water. The Oilers would have been safer living on a landfill. By practicing on the germ-infested field, players' minor scratches became easily infected. Every morning players lined up outside the training room for shots of antibiotics.

Naturally, the stench from the sewer-watered field was gut-wrenching. But by then, the veterans were getting used to it. After all, the previous Oiler training camps stunk, too—in more ways than one.

DICK TOMEY

Coach • University of Hawaii Rainbow Warriors • August, 1985

Dick Tomey's 1985 training camp ignited the Hawaii players with a burning desire to win that bordered on lunacy.

Tomey entered his team in a seminar on personal development and motivation. But this six-hour session, purporting to "turn fear into power," was far from ordinary. To make sure the players understood the message, they were given a test. They had to walk over hot coals—barefoot.

About 90 men on Tomey's 120-man squad actually stepped barefoot through a 12-foot-long bed of glowing red coals, making the Warriors the football team with the most bizarre method for getting fired up.

The purpose of the fire walk was to "enrich the educational experience, not to go 12–0," said Tomey. "This will help our players in the classroom, personal life and may even help us as a team, although we have no delusions it will make us a great football team."

It didn't even make the Rainbow Warriors a good team. Hawaii was raked over the coals for a 4–6–2 record.

JOE KUHARICH

Coach • University of San Francisco Dons • August, 1950

Joe Kuharich was called "the Barracuda." That was much too nice a name for a coach whose brutal training camp would have wiped out the entire Foreign Legion.

For pre-season conditioning, he forced his team to practice in the searing desert heat in Corning, California, where the summer temperatures hovered near a sizzling 115 degrees. Perhaps this choice of training camp would have made some sense if the Dons had scheduled their home games in the Sahara.

There was no sense in Kuharich's ungodly custom of withholding water from his parched players. Because he thought it was bad for conditioning, he didn't want anyone drinking water, so he added oatmeal to the team's water bucket! "It was like a rotten kind of mouthwash that you couldn't swallow," recalled Bill Henneberry, a former player who lived to tell about it. "Every time you tried to take a drink, you had to spit it out."

Kuharich himself once described how his waterless regimen nearly killed a burly fullback. "He got into a crouch and just froze there—he'd lost all the salt in his body. For a while, we thought he'd had it."

Kuharich turned his dehydrated players into human raisins. During five hours of daily practice, they just withered up in the scorching heat. "We damned near died," said Henneberry. "He drove the hell out of us. The only shade we found came from the light poles around the field. It looked so funny. You'd see us guys in a line all trying to stand along a one-foot-wide shadow."

But there were precious few minutes when the players had the chance to stand still. "Joe had us running day and night," recalled running back Ollie Matson, who pulled through the coach's deadly training camps and went on to a Hall of Fame career as a pro. "He made you run and you didn't stop until he told you. But sometimes he'd get so engrossed in something else that he'd forget about you until you dropped."

One of Kuharich's favorite practice drills was a sadistic version of "King of the Hill." Two players would face each other at the top of a steep hill and try to knock each other over the edge. "Believe me, it was one long climb back up after you rolled all the way to the bottom," said Matson.

Running backs were forced to run through a bruising gauntlet of players. Like frightened jackrabbits, the runners tried to duck, dodge, and weave their way through to safety while everybody else took pot-shots at them.

"Many of us had just come out of the Army and the physical training we had in the service was nothing compared to what Joe put us through," said Matson. One of the players was rough, tough future Hall of Famer Gino Marchetti. Even though he had fought in the Battle of the Bulge and had endured all the horrors of war, he still wasn't prepared for Kuharich's cruel training camp. After two weeks of agony, even Marchetti had had enough, and screamed, "Get me out of here! Get me out of here!"

Said Matson, "It's the kind of hell you never forget."

LARRY JONES

Coach ▪ Florida State Seminoles ▪ 1973

In its ever-vigilant fight to rid the world of human rights violations, Amnesty International somehow overlooked "The Room," Larry Jones' torture chamber.

The horrors concocted in The Room by the twisted minds of the Florida State coaching staff were so inhumane that twenty-eight scholarship players—nearly twenty-five percent of the entire team—quit football rather than subject themselves to such needless brutality.

The Room was a former varsity dressing area stripped of all lockers and other furniture. Four feet above a floor of mats, chicken wire was hung horizontally across the room. In this confining enclosure, the players endured cruel, gruelling agility drills and bloody one-on-one, knock-down-drag-out fights.

Before the start of spring drills, Jones violated NCAA rules by ordering his players to take a special nine-week physical education class that was nothing more than a series of illegal—and barbarous—practice sessions. Four times a week, the players reported for two hours of what one team official later admitted was "the most brutal, demoralizing, depersonalizing thing any kid could go through."

In The Room, the coaching staff took up positions around the chicken wire enclosure and screamed at, cursed, and struck the players as they performed exhausting drills from a stooped position.

The staff mentality sank to the level of cock fight spectators when the coaches pitted teammate against teammate in bloody, vicious, hand-to-hand combat. The coaches encouraged the winners to yell and swear at their opponents and try to draw blood.

"The only rule was that no one could hit below the belt," recalled Hod Verble, one of the Florida State scholarship players who quit. "Two players would line up back-to-back and a coach would blow his whistle. Then the players would turn around and just start hitting. I've seen people with blood completely covering their shirts. You could be standing there puking blood and the coaches would just holler louder, 'Get tough! Get tough!' "

Losers were forced to wrestle until they won, which meant that small, lightweight backs often had to battle huge, bruising linemen. "The coaches made no attempt to separate the smaller players from the bigger ones," said Verble.

The final wrestling loser of the day joined any other players who were punished for various offenses and reported to the stadium at 6:30 A.M. on Fridays. There, they had to run up the ninety or so steps of the stadium and then back down again from ten to twenty times without stopping.

The coaching staff claimed The Room built character. Actually, all it built was a winless team. Florida State lost every one of its 11 games that fall. Coach Jones resigned in disgrace and the NCAA put the school on probation for one year.

The only person who would have fully appreciated The Room was Edgar Allan Poe, whose tales of horror were mild in comparison with Jones'.

BOOB TUBE BOOBS

Television network executives don't always focus in on the best interests of the football fan. They make so many brainless programming decisions they should be penalized for roughing the viewers. Somebody ought to pull the plug on these nitwits. For "The Most Foolish Actions by TV Networks," The Football Hall of SHAME inducts the following:

NBC'S *HEIDI* FIASCO

Nov. 17, 1968

NBC had a decision to make: continue to telecast a dramatic football game that was running late or cut away to the scheduled special, the classic *Heidi*.

In one of the greatest travesties of televised sports history, the network lost all sense of priorities and ruled in favor of the little children of America.

For three hours, millions of football fans across the country sat on the edge of their seats, mesmerized by the thrilling seesaw battle between the AFL's defending champion Oakland Raiders and Joe Namath's high-flying New York Jets. The game was not only exciting, but also important, because both teams were fighting for divisional titles.

When Jim Turner booted New York into a 32–29 lead on a 26-yard field goal with 65 seconds left, it looked like a Jets victory. But the Raiders, known for their heart-stopping comebacks, roared to the New York 43-yard line. It was first-and-ten with 50 seconds remaining.

It was also 7 P.M. That's when a network executive decided to push some buttons. Suddenly, a commercial came on the TV screen. When it ended, the climax to the Raiders-Jets game did not reappear. Instead, a

Swiss miss named Heidi was being asked by this nice man to please come live with his ailing daughter.

Irate football fans exploded in a nationwide apoplectic fit. The NBC switchboard in New York lit up with so many calls of protest that its fuses blew. The fans also vented their outrage with calls to newspapers, radio stations, NBC affiliates, and even the New York Police Department, managing to tie up be the most elaborate municipal emergency call system in the world. Meanwhile, mothers all over the country tried to hush angry fathers who, in front of the children, were loudly badmouthing a nice little girl like Heidi.

What did the fans miss? Not much—just 2 last-second Oakland touch-downs. On the very next play after the network left the game, Daryle Lamonica threw a 43-yard TD pass to Charlie Smith. Then, on the ensuing kickoff, the Jets' Earl Christy fumbled the ball in the end zone, where Raider Preston Ridlehuber recovered it for another Oakland touchdown. Final score: Raiders 43, Jets 32.

The network tried to ease fan frustration by running streamers, giving the score of the game at the bottom of the TV screen. But NBC couldn't even do this right. Rather than wait until there was a lull in the story, the network flashed a streamer during a particularly poignant moment in the drama. Thus, viewers were seeing the score while in the background Heidi's partially paralyzed cousin Klara was summoning enough courage to try to walk.

At least NBC admitted its goof. Pleasing football fans everywhere, it said that the next time the network had to choose between Joe Namath and Heidi, the little orphan girl would be left out in the cold.

NBC'S FIRST TELEVISED FOOTBALL GAME

Oct. 22, 1939

Excited viewers crowded around New York City's 1,000 television sets in happy anticipation of pro football's first televised game, a clash between the Philadelphia Eagles and the Brooklyn Dodgers at Ebbets Field.

The fans at home were psyched up. No longer would they have to listen to the game on the radio. They would actually get to *see* the action on TV. At least, that's what the viewers and crew of NBC station W2XBS thought.

Before the game was over, however, the fans had a dim view of the pioneer broadcast. In fact, there were times when they had no view at all. They were reduced to listening to the game, just as they had before; only this time the broadcast came from their darkened TV sets.

NBC hadn't counted on the effects of the weather. Every time a cloud rolled in front of the sun, the picture on the TV screen grew darker because there wasn't enough light for the two iconoscope cameras. As the day turned increasingly cloudy, the picture often went completely blank, forcing sportscaster Allan Walz to deliver a play-by-play more suited to radio.

ABC'S *SUPERDOME*
Jan. 9, 1978

CBS'S *BLACK SUNDAY*
Jan. 21, 1979

In a stroke of mindless programming, both ABC and CBS waited until Super Bowl week to telecast two exploitative, violent TV movies revolving around football's annual showcase event.

Hoping to score a ratings coup, each network ignored any moral concern over the broadcasts' potential for triggering mayhem at the game. Even more frightening, both movies chillingly illustrated what easy targets our huge stadiums are for the madmen of the world.

In 1978, six days before Super Bowl XII was played in the Louisiana Superdome, ABC witlessly ran the made-for-TV movie *Superdome,* a cutthroat drama saturated with murderers and gamblers bent on fixing the game.

NFL commissioner Pete Rozelle appropriately decried the telecast as "ill-timed" and "in poor taste." Concerned over its impact on the minds of unstable viewers, Rozelle warned: "The power of suggestion in things like this is so great."

How true. Two days after ABC broadcast *Superdome,* the Denver Broncos received a telephone threat on the life of their star running back, John Keyworth. Strict security measures were immediately invoked by the team as it prepared for its Super Bowl showdown with the Dallas Cowboys. An armed guard was posted outside Keyworth's hotel room. Keyworth admitted he was "a little shook up" over the incident. Fortunately, the threat was never carried out.

The next year, CBS fueled its ongoing quest to top ABC whenever possible—even in senselessness. CBS had the audacity to plan its telecast

of the terrorist film *Black Sunday* in prime time shortly after the final gun sounded at Super Bowl XIII. Throughout the week before the game, viewers were assaulted with hype about the movie, in which Arab guerrillas plan to bomb the Super Bowl and send all 80,000 attending fans to kingdom come.

In the film, Marthe Keller portrays a beautiful but lethal Palestinian who teams up with Lander, a disturbed former Vietnam War POW, played by Bruce Dern. As a brilliant explosives expert and crack pilot who flies the Goodyear blimp, Lander designs a bomb that will drop from the blimp as it floats over the Orange Bowl during the big game between the Pittsburgh Steelers and the Dallas Cowboys.

As luck would have it, the movie was being ballyhooed all week on CBS while the Steelers and the Cowboys were, in fact, in the Orange Bowl—in Super Bowl XIII.

Before the kickoff, a squad of explosives experts with specially trained dogs examined every square inch of the stadium. Fortunately, the only bomb seen that day was CBS' telecast of *Black Sunday*.

NBC'S ANNOUNCERLESS TELECAST

Dec. 20, 1980

Silence may often be golden, but on television it is less than sterling. To attract viewers to an otherwise meaningless season-ending contest between the New York Jets (3–12) and the Miami Dolphins (8–7) in the Orange Bowl, NBC tried an experiment. The network telecast the game without announcers.

Shushing the play-by-play proved too hard on the viewers—especially on their brains, eyes, stomachs, and bladders.

After the first few minutes, the novelty of silence wore off. The sparse, no-frills broadcast required intense concentration from viewers, who began to feel like they were working instead of enjoying the game. Viewers, used to being spoon-fed information by sportscasters, were forced to spend the afternoon glued to the screen. They had to constantly read graphics and statistics in order to keep up with the game's developments. By halftime, their eyes started spinning in their heads because of the numbing number of graphics.

Viewers didn't dare walk away from their TV sets for a stretch, a snack, or a trip to the bathroom for fear of missing something important. At least by listening to an announcer, you can do any of those things and still stay abreast of the action.

Absence made the viewers' hearts grow fonder for announcers. Without the play-by-play and commentary, there was no way to provide anecdotal background that humanizes players and coaches; no way to keep track of substitutions; no way to tell who threw the key block; no way to build drama at critical points, and no way to put replays and developments into perspective.

NBC had hoped to make up at least partly for the empty broadcast booth by using twelve special microphones to pick up the noise of the crowd and the sound of combat on the field. The enhanced audio was supposed to create a sense of immediacy, of being there. But the acoustics in the Orange Bowl swallowed up the sound. NBC's sophisticated microphones couldn't pick up the crunch of the bodies, the grunts of the players, or the quarterbacks' barking of signals. There was no audio problem, however, when it came time for the annoying commercials.

The announcerless telecast didn't work because, as sports commentator Pete Axthelm said, "Drama needs words like music needs lyrics."

The lesson NBC learned from the silent telecast came through loud and clear: Don't try it again.

SUBSTANDARD BEARERS

Football players set examples for kids, but, unfortunately, not all examples are good ones. Imagine what might happen if youngsters emulated some of the game's most woeful "heroes," those rogues, crackpots, and wild cards who seem to live each day out of bounds. These kids would likely grow up to become as successful as the World Football League. For "The Sorriest Role Models for America's Youth," The Football Hall of SHAME inducts the following:

JOE NAMATH

Quarterback ▪ New York Jets ▪ February–March, 1974

Joe Namath knocked the socks off his incredulous fans when he modeled panty hose on a network television commercial. What sheer audacity!

Suddenly their hero, football's macho man, had become the darling of America's transvestites.

How could this be? Joe Willie had spent years in the discos, bars, and bedrooms, building his reputation as the sports world's No. 1 lady-killer. In July 1970, he showed fans that women were more important to him than his own teammates were. While the rest of the New York Jets were broiling alive during two-a-days in training camp, Namath was squiring starlets in Hollywood and shooting a movie. The front page of the *New York Daily News* once showed him doing a love scene with the luscious Ann-Margret for the movie *C.C. and Company*. The back page of the same edition displayed a photo of his teammates, who were sweating and working themselves into shape for the upcoming season.

But in early 1974, Namath fans began moaning, "Say it ain't so, Joe!"—a refrain that, until his panty hose commercial, had belonged solely to baseball.

The commercial, which ran repeatedly for two months on the networks and then in thirty major markets, started out by slowly panning up a pair of attractive, shaved legs. Off-camera, a female voice said, "This commercial is going to prove to the women of America that Beautymist Panty Hose can make anybody's legs look like a million dollars." Then the camera showed a pair of green shorts, a Jets jersey, and finally a grinning Joe Namath, who said, "If Beautymist can make my legs look this good, think what they can do for yours."

Think what they did do to the psyche of Namath's young hero-worshippers who, until his hose job, had no doubts about emulating him. Kids were especially confused since the commercial ran after Namath's manager, Jimmy Walsh, told the press, "Joe won't advertise any product he doesn't approve of, live with or use."

Namath, who commanded fees of six and seven figures to pitch everything from popcorn poppers to pillowcases, was the hottest celebrity seller on TV at the time. He was approached by the Long, Haymes & Carr, Inc. advertising agency to appear in the tongue-in-cheek commercial for Beautymist, a brand of the Hanes Hosiery division of Sara Lee. "We worried about doing the commercial," said Walsh. "We had to be sure there was no hint of effeminacy in it. We insisted on having a beautiful model kiss him at the end of the commercial to reaffirm his masculinity."

Most fans wanted to believe Namath was still macho. But one thing bothered them. Namath's legs *did* look awfully good in panty hose.

JOE DON LOONEY

Running Back–Punter • Baltimore Colts–Detroit Lions– Washington Redskins–New Orleans Saints • 1964–69

Never was a football player more aptly named than Joe Don Looney.

In the gridiron of life, he was born on the 51-yard-line. He was a loose ball that no one could handle. Known as "Football's Marvelous Misfit," Looney possessed a talent matched only by his intense dislike for conformity and authority. He refused to take orders from coaches, assistant coaches, general managers, quarterbacks, and trainers alike. He wouldn't even throw his dirty towels into the right locker room bin because, he declared, "No stupid sign is gonna tell me what to do."

As the No. 1 draft choice for the New York Giants in 1964, Looney had all the moves, power, and speed to make him a great running back. But he quickly fumbled away the greatness that was in him.

No sooner had he arrived at the Giants training camp than he drew a fine for refusing to have his ankles taped before scrimmages. "I know my ankles better than you do," he told the trainer. When Looney thought a team meeting was pointless, he simply didn't show up. Naturally, he was fined. Slapped with another fine for missing curfew by ten minutes, Looney protested that he had checked in an hour earlier the previous night and reasoned "they owe me fifty minutes."

In scrimmages, he ran plays his way and not as diagrammed. "Anybody can run where the hole is," he said. "A good football player makes his own holes." Out on the practice field, Looney preferred to play catch with a nine-year-old fan rather than work out with Giants quarterback Y.A. Tittle. Looney soon piled up so many fines that he couldn't afford to play for the Giants.

His days on the team were numbered, especially after he informed coach Allie Sherman that he wasn't going to practice anymore.

"Why not?" asked the incredulous coach, trying to control his temper.

"I know the plays," answered the smug 6-foot, 2-inch, 230-pound running back. "It doesn't make any sense for me to go out there and run around doing stuff I've already learned. Let me know when you're going to get into something new."

Fighting the urge to kill, the infuriated coach enlisted the aid of Tittle, the Giants' elder statesman, to talk some sense into the brash rookie. An hour after chatting with Looney, Tittle went to Sherman and said, "I didn't get anywhere with him, Al. But you know something? He makes sense. I know all the plays, too. Why should I have to practice?"

Sherman realized that the only way to stop such blasphemy was to get rid of Looney, so the Giants shipped him to the Baltimore Colts after only twenty-eight days in training camp. Before leaving, Looney took out his frustration on a recoil blocking dummy by smashing it with his shoulder. The dummy recoiled and knocked Looney on his butt. Joe Don went berserk and attacked the dummy—punching, kicking, and swearing at it.

Although he seemed to improve his attitude with the Colts, Looney nevertheless showed undisciplined stubbornness. Coach Don Shula hesitated to send Looney in as a punter because Shula just couldn't be sure that Looney would even kick the ball on fourth down. So Looney was shipped off to the Detroit Lions.

At first they tolerated the problem child who once said, "I never met a man I didn't like—except Will Rogers." The Lions began to worry when Looney showed up in the locker room with a puppy loaded down with weights. Looney explained to his curious teammates that he was trying to build up the dog's leg muscles. Both he and his dog shared snacks of wheat germ and sunflower seeds, Looney added.

The Lions front office grew tired of Looney's antics when he refused to report to practice one day. Trying to straighten out the wayward player, assistant coach Joe Schmidt offered him some simple advice: "You've got to work hard in this league. I've been with the club for twelve years, and I've never missed a practice."

"Joe, you should take a day off once in a while," replied Looney—who was promptly suspended for a few days.

Lions coach Harry Gilmer finally lost his patience with Looney during a 1966 game against the Atlanta Falcons. Just before the half, Gilmer wanted to send Looney into the game with a play for quarterback Milt Plum to run. Looney refused. "If you want a messenger," said Looney, heading back to the bench, "call Western Union." Gilmer didn't even wait for the game to end to take action. He suspended Looney at halftime.

Once again, Joe Don was in trouble. It was the same old Looney tune.

TOM "HOLLYWOOD" HENDERSON

Linebacker ▪ Dallas Cowboys ▪ 1975–79

The most tasteless hot dog in football was Hollywood Henderson. His self-serving boasts, low-blow knocks, and attention-getting antics during games were just too much to swallow.

Henderson grew a mouth as big as a football field—with an ego to match—when he played at Langston College in Oklahoma. He certainly didn't endear himself to his teammates, constantly reminding them how great he was and how lousy they were. To show Henderson how they felt, they began taking cheap shots at him during practice. As a result, the coach decided that it was in Henderson's best interests not to play him much in practice scrimmages.

No one was surprised when Henderson held a press conference to praise himself after the Dallas Cowboys drafted him in the first round in 1975. Neither were they startled when he christened himself "Hollywood" in recognition of what he called his showmanship. He talked a much better game than he played, grabbing more headlines than interceptions.

A few days before his first Super Bowl in 1976, he fell asleep during a team meeting, then bragged that he was tired because he had gone out the night before with the Pointer Sisters.

Before the 1978 NFC championship game against the Los Angeles

Rams, Henderson showed a complete lack of respect for his opponents by announcing, "The Rams don't have enough class to make it to the Super Bowl. If the Rams don't choke, I will choke them." To underscore his rap, he stood in the middle of the field at the end of the pre-game warmup, faced the Rams, and clutched his throat with both hands in an exaggerated gesture.

In the fourth quarter, with Dallas leading 21–0, Henderson intercepted a pass and ran 65 yards for the Cowboys' final touchdown. He applied the coup de grace by jumping high up to the crossbar and laying the ball over the bar with a finger roll. But rather than stop there, he wanted to rub it in. He trotted to the sidelines and picked up a blue and gold Ram pom-pom. He gave a mock cheer and then tore the pom-pom to shreds. Later in the game, he stood on the field, pointing a finger at Los Angeles Coach Ray Malavasi, and taunted, "Hurts, don't it, Malavasi?"

Henderson was just warming up his mouth for Super Bowl XIII. Throughout the week, he became so overexposed and overquoted that fans were overdosing on his babble. He insulted the intelligence of opposing quarterback Terry Bradshaw of the Pittsburgh Steelers, claiming, "He couldn't spell cat if you spotted him the 'c' and the 'a.'" Then Henderson lashed out at Steeler tight end Randy Grossman, saying,

"How much respect can you have for a backup? Grossman only plays when somebody dies or breaks a leg. He's the last hope."

The following season, in 1979, Henderson got too "Hollywood" for his own good. First, he arrived at training camp in a chauffeured limousine. Then he goofed off in practice. "I don't need to practice," he announced. "I'd do just as well if they would mail me the game plan every week."

By midseason, Henderson had missed several practices and games because of unconfirmed ailments. He didn't miss any opportunities to attract the TV cameras, however. The "injured" player showed up on the sidelines in a full-length mink coat. When he did play, he was terrible, and repeatedly got burned on touchdown passes.

Dallas coach Tom Landry finally sacked Henderson—after a crushing 34–20 loss to the Washington Redskins—because he had played the role of clown, rather than linebacker, once too often. In the game, Henderson had been shut out—he had no tackles, no assists, and no contributions of any kind. When the Redskins had built up an insurmountable lead, a sideline camera revealed just how much his poor performance had troubled the cocky linebacker. He horsed around behind the bench, mugged for the camera, and pointed to his crotch, where a bandana dangling from his waist said "Dallas No. 1." In the press box, the Dallas assistant coaches, who viewed his act on TV monitors, were outraged. So was Landry.

The next day, Landry called Henderson into his office and fired him. The game of football was spared any more sorry Hollywood tales.

JOHN RIGGINS

Fullback · Washington Redskins · Jan. 31, 1985

No player was ever more offside than John Riggins was when he attended the Washington Press Club's annual Salute to Congress.

Before the night was over, Riggins had insulted the Vice-President of the United States, the governor of Virginia, and the country's first woman Supreme Court justice. Then, the 240-pound fullback passed out on the floor.

For his deplorable performance, Riggins made headlines—but not the kind his young fans should have been reading.

When it came to civility, Riggins fumbled the ball at the black tie dinner. Sitting at the table with Supreme Court Justice Sandra Day O'Connor, Riggins asked her when she would pose for a pinup poster.

When she didn't laugh, he told her, "Loosen up, baby...You're too tight."

Grabbing one of the helium balloons floating over the table, Riggins sucked in the balloon's gas and talked like Donald Duck for the politely smiling but embarrassed group. He passed the balloon to Virginia Governor Charles Robb, who demurred. Later, when the conversation turned to heroes, Riggins yelled to Robb, "You're no hero, you're the . . . governor."

At one point during the $65-a-plate dinner, Riggins jumped up and started kicking the seat of his chair. Depending on which guest you believe, Riggins was either trying to fix the chair, destroy the chair, or clear off the salad that he had dropped on his lap.

Just before the speeches began, Riggins threw his formal bow tie across the table and unbuttoned the top of his shirt. He made his way around the table, as if to bid farewell, then dropped to the floor where he slept for the next hour—missing several speeches, including one by Vice-President George Bush. While asleep, Riggins kept flopping his head onto the foot of guest Annie Glenn, wife of Senator John Glenn of Ohio. Mrs. Glenn was so outraged she moved to another table.

When he was awakened after the speeches, Riggins got up slowly, his face pale and perspiring, and was escorted out of the ballroom by two editors from *People* magazine, which had invited Riggins to the swank affair.

When photos and stories about his boorish behavior appeared the next day, Riggins' image had been thrown for another loss.

WORLD FOOTBALL LEAGUE

1974–75

It barely occupies a footnote in the history book of sports enterprises, but the World Football League still stands as a shameful monument to the most unsuccessful football venture ever formed.

The WFL died, before it was two years old, of financial starvation brought on by mindless mismanagement, meager resources, pitiful attendance, and lousy playing. The players faced no pay days, no pay weeks, and even no pay *months*. Ultimately, the teams were awash in a sea of red ink, with debts and losses that totaled an estimated $30 million.

In the summer of 1974, league founder Gary Davidson and his supporters predicted the World Football League would truly live up to its name, eventually fielding expansion teams around the globe. Why, even the Dalai Lama himself was rumored to want a franchise for Tibet.

To the surprise of everyone, including the starry-eyed optimists, attendance figures soared in the league's first few weeks. The Philadelphia Bell worried the established NFL sick when the team announced crowds of 55,534 and 64,719 for its first two games.

But when the Bell's third game drew only 12, 396 fans, the "Philadelphia Paper Gate Scandal" broke wide open. The Bell confessed it had papered the house for the first two games. It had sold 31,800 tickets for its opener and just 6,200 for the second game. Everyone else had gotten in free. Presumably, management let the fans in gratis in the hopes that they would pay to get out.

Suddenly, stories were surfacing almost daily about league troubles, as one team after another began losing credibility—and money. In the WFL's first season, more than two-thirds of the players weren't paid full salaries. In one common tale of woe, players who were released by the league's Hawaiian franchise didn't have the money for air fare to the mainland and home.

The owners were getting more press than the players. The Jacksonville Sharks went belly-up, but not before owner Fran Manaco managed to meet one payroll by borrowing $27,000 from head coach Bud Asher—whom he then fired, probably for displaying such bad judgment in loaning money to the owner. Some of the out-of-work players threatened to file fraud-and-deceit suits against team management and league officials.

The Southern California Sun bankrupted their first owner. The man who then bailed them out soon had to be bailed out himself, when he pleaded guilty to making false statements in order to obtain bank financing.

In Detroit, the Wheels franchise was awarded to a hospital employee named Bud Hucul, whose previous business ventures had netted him thirty arrests and twenty-seven lawsuits. His players quickly learned that the Wheels were out of financial alignment when the teams ran out of adhesive tape and had to borrow some from opposing teams. The Wheels were too broke to replace busted shoelaces, film their games, or print up programs. When they couldn't get their uniforms out of the laundry because they had failed to pay the bill, practice was cancelled. Needless to say, the team didn't fare much better on the field than off, winning only 3 of 12 games. During the second half of one home game, the few fans in the stands amused themselves by playing Frisbee. When the public address announcer said, "The Wheels will play out of town next week," spectators cheered. Midway through the first season, the Wheels disbanded, leaving a list of 122 creditors.

The Houston Texans, who couldn't even come up with a $14,000 deposit to secure a lease to play at Rice Stadium, folded early in the first season. The team's legacy was summed up nicely by a Houston sportswriter, who said, "The Texans left town just like they came—broke, disorganized and unwanted." The team was rechristened the Steamer and found a new home in Shreveport, Louisiana. Interestingly, not one of the five WFL teams that came to Shreveport to play was able to pay its hotel bill.

The New York Stars suffered a housing problem. Without any big bucks, they were forced to play at cheap Triborough Stadium on Randalls Island—the Alcatraz of football. The lights were so bad the players should have used lighted coal miners' helmets to see inside the 20-yard lines. One wag claimed, "The Stars play at Triborough Stadium with eight small candles strategically placed, four on each side of the stadium." The Stars sought a brighter future elsewhere and, thirteen weeks into the season, moved to Charlotte, North Carolina.

Before the WFL's first season ended, founder Gary Davidson was fired and the play-off system was revised three times. The Chicago Fire, eligible for a shot at the play-offs, declined to play their final game when their owner threw in the towel.

Like compulsive gamblers who don't know when to stop, the surviving owners rolled the dice again for a second season. The dice came up snake eyes.

On October 22, 1975, in the twelfth week of the second year, the record-setting money loser of a league collapsed. Left in the rubble of unpaid bills were 380 players suddenly without jobs.

When word reached the California Sun, the players headed for a tavern and rallied around twenty-seven pitchers of beer. In a fitting end to the league, the athletes who had played, sweated, and bled together got sloshed together.

JIM McMAHON

Quarterback • Chicago Bears • Jan. 22, 1986

If ever a pro quarterback was born to be wild, it was Jim McMahon.

From the time he showed up at his first Chicago Bears press conference with a can of beer in his hand, he has been predictably unpredictable. With his punk-rock sunglasses, butch haircuts, sideline head-butts, and "message" headbands, football's bad boy sure knows how to shake, rattle, and roll out. The world has come to know him as the poster child for the terminally flaky.

During Super Bowl week, McMahon revealed a new—but not an altogether surprising—side of himself. In front of the press and with a helicopter overhead, he dropped his pants, bent over, and showed his ass, triggering a debate over whether or not he was one.

McMahon had been suffering a pain in his private backfield from a hit he had taken in the NFC championship game ten days earlier. Amid great fanfare, he flew his acupuncturist, Hiroshi Shiriashi, to New Orleans, the site of Super Bowl XX, to see what Shiriashi could do to help. At the start of practice four days before the big game, McMahon wore a headband that read, "ACUPUNCTURE." When he noticed a helicopter hovering overhead, he decided to show off the sorest part of his anatomy to the passing copter and the horde of photographers who were tailing him. Some newspapers ran a revealing photograph of this historic moment on the front page of their sports sections, causing some fans to wonder if McMahon was a Chicago Bear or a Chicago Bare.

McMahon's moon put New Orleans' image as the Crescent City in fresh perspective. It also put him in the slimelight in the eyes of some unamused feminists, who were already upset by a report—later proven untrue—that he had called the city's women "sluts." A score of female protesters mobilized in front of the Bears' hotel and carried a banner that read, "McMAHON HAS NO CLASS. HE ONLY SHOWS HIS ASS."

THE FUMBLE FOLLIES

You can tell who they are by looking at their fingers—they're all thumbs. These players are the maladroit bumblers who carry the ball as if they are allergic to pigskin. Their muffs often trigger a rash of boos and jeers that stay with them longer than the ball. For "The Most Outrageous Fumbles," The Football Hall of SHAME inducts the following:

JACK CONCANNON

Quarterback · Chicago Bears · Sept. 28, 1969

In one of the most embarrassing fumbles ever committed in a pro football game, Chicago Bears quarterback Jack Concannon coughed up the football after calling time out.

The foolish fumble occurred in the first quarter of a game with the St. Louis Cardinals, when the Bears were faced with a first-and-ten at the Cardinal 34-yard line. In the huddle, Concannon called the play, telling center Mike Pyle to snap the ball on a quick count. "Do it on the first sound you hear," said Concannon.

As the teams lined up, Concannon assumed his position behind Pyle, but then noticed that one of his Bear teammates was not in the right place for the play. Concannon suddenly backed away, formed a "T" with his hands, and shouted, "Time out!"

But Pyle, being the good center that he was, had followed orders. He snapped the ball on the very first sound he heard—even though it wasn't quite what he expected. The ball bounced off the quarterback's knee and spurted 20 feet straight up. Like a shortstop racing in to catch a bunted pop-up, Cardinal linebacker Larry Stallings caught the ball on the dead run and rambled 62 yards into the end zone for his very first career touchdown.

Nobody even chased him. Other than Pyle, all the Bears had heeded Concannon's call for time out and didn't move. Unfortunately for them, Stallings wasn't paying attention to Concannon, and the play unfolded before the referee could react to the time-out request.

The fumble was not only mortifying, but costly as well, because the touchdown it generated proved to be the margin of defeat. The Bears lost 20–17.

OAKLAND RAIDERS

Sept. 10, 1978

In the most shameful fumble in pro football history, the Oakland Raiders deliberately dropped the ball, then batted and kicked it into the end zone for a last-ditch, game-saving touchdown.

"The play is in our playbook," bragged Oakland guard Gene Upshaw after the contest. "It's called 'Win At Any Cost.'"

Trailing the San Diego Chargers 20–14 with only 10 seconds left in the game, the Raiders desperately needed to score a touchdown. Oakland quarterback Ken Stabler took the center snap at the San Diego 14-yard line and looked for a receiver. Just as he realized nobody was open, Stabler was hit from his blind side for what looked like a game-ending sack.

But, with a flick of his wrist, the crafty veteran fumbled the ball forward. It bounded to the 8-yard line, where Oakland's Pete Banaszak—in an Oscar-worthy portrayal of a klutz—batted and booted the ball to the goal line. There, teammate Dave Casper kicked it into the end zone and then fell on it for the tying touchdown. The point-after, which came after time had expired, gave the Raiders a victory they did not deserve.

After the game, the three Oakland players admitted it had been a phony fumble. "I tried to fumble," said Stabler. "If I get sacked, the game is over." Said Banaszak, "Sure I batted it. I could see a San Diego guy right alongside me. If I picked it up, he would have tackled me and the game would have been over." Added Casper, "Sure, I helped the ball along into the end zone."

What the Raiders did was illegal, but the NFL said it was impossible for the officials to judge "intent" since Stabler, Banaszak, and Casper conveniently waited until after the game was over to confess.

To make sure the fake fumble didn't appear in any team's playbook the following year, the league added a new rule that states: "Any fumble that occurs during a down after the two-minute warning may not be advanced by any member of the fumbling team except the player who fumbled the ball."

That did little to soothe the outrage of San Diego fans. They showed their feelings by wearing T-shirts that displayed a blindfolded referee signaling a touchdown with the words, "IMMACULATE DECEPTION."

EAST CAROLINA PIRATES

Sept. 13, 1980

It's nice to be magnanimous, but the East Carolina Pirates were generous to a fault.

They kept giving away the football. In fact, they fumbled on 5 straight possessions in one quarter to set a collegiate mark in botchery. They gave until it hurt. And all they had to show for their generosity was a stinging defeat.

The Southwestern Louisiana Ragin' Cajuns were the recipients of the Pirates' charity. Highly favored ECU was leading 7–3 at the start of the third quarter when the team revealed why it should have changed its name from Pirates to Philanthropists.

The second half was less than a minute old when quarterback Carlton Nelson and running back Theodore Sutton bungled the handoff and lost the ball on their 35-yard line. Six plays later, the Ragin' Cajuns took a 10–7 lead.

Believing one good turnover deserves another, Nelson coughed up the ball again 3 plays after the ensuing kickoff. Recovering on the ECU 42-yard line, Southwestern Louisiana drove into the end zone, making the score 17–7.

The Pirates wasted little time doling out more gifts. On their third possession of the period, Nelson fumbled away the ball on the Ragin' Cajuns' 41-yard line. But the Cajuns couldn't exchange the gift for a score, and punted.

Two plays later, however, ECU bestowed the football upon Southwestern Louisiana when running back Mike Hawkins fumbled on his 20-yard line. The Ragin' Cajuns took full advantage of the endowment for a 24–7 lead.

The Pirates' largess knew no bounds. For the fifth straight possession, they turned the ball over, this time when a punt slipped through the hands of returner Willie Holley on the ECU 19-yard line. Southwestern Louisiana cashed the miscue in for a field goal that boosted the margin to 27–7 as the fourth quarter began.

All but 3 of the Cajuns' 27 points came as a result of Pirate presents. Yet when the Ragin' Cajuns walked off the field 27–21 victors, they didn't even say thank you.

NEW YORK GIANTS

Nov. 19, 1978

The New York Giants were beating the Philadelphia Eagles 17–12. Only 28 seconds remained and the clock was running because the Eagles had used up their final time-out. The Giants faced a third-and-two situation at their own 29-yard line. All they had to do was fall on the ball, and the victory was theirs.

There was no way they could lose—except one possibility so far-fetched that even the most hopeless pessimist would admit it couldn't happen. But, impossible as it seems, it did.

As the clock ticked off the final seconds, New York's offensive coordinator Bob Gibson sent in the play "Pro 65 Up," calling for fullback Larry Csonka to run over left guard. Most of the Giants in the huddle were incredulous. They yelled at quarterback Joe Pisarcik to change the call, simply fall on the ball, and take no chances with a missed handoff. It all made sense. Even if the Giants did not make a first down, time would run out before they were required to run another play. But Pisarcik,

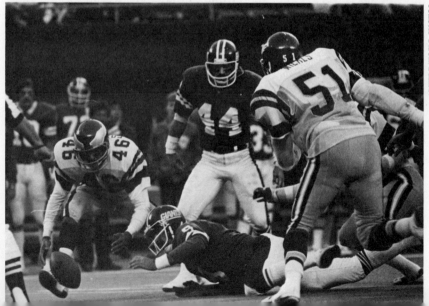

reprimanded by Coach Gibson in the past for not following his orders, ran the play—or rather attempted to run it.

As Pisarcik took the center snap and pivoted to make the handoff, he lost control of the ball. It bounced off Csonka's hip and hit the artificial turf at Giants Stadium. Eagle defender Herman Edwards couldn't believe his eyes. He scooped up the loose ball and jubilantly ran untouched into the end zone—with just 20 seconds left in the game—for an unbelievable 19–17 Philadelphia victory.

"That's the most horrifying ending to a ball game I've ever seen," lamented shaken New York head coach John McVay.

When the Giants lost the game, assistant coach Gibson lost his job.

DAVE SMITH

Wide Receiver • Pittsburgh Steelers • Oct. 18, 1971

A funny thing happened to Dave Smith on his way toward an easy touchdown. He lost this inhibitions, his dignity, his sanity—and the ball.

It all happened on the most bungled spike ever witnessed by a national TV audience.

During the fourth quarter of a Monday night game won by the Kansas City Chiefs, 38–16, Smith caught a pass from Pittsburgh Steelers quarterback Terry Bradshaw and broke through a crowded field of defenders. Smith zigzagged his way toward the end zone for what appeared to be a 55-yard touchdown pass play.

But suddenly, he was struck with an irresistible urge to celebrate his feat. Smith raised the ball above his head in the opening gesture of the classic spike. Unfortunately, his timing was off. In his eagerness to slam the ball to the turf, he failed to notice that he had yet to cross the goal line. As he streaked to the 5-yard line, the ball slipped out of his outstretched hand and bounded all the way through the end zone.

The touchdown turned into a touchback. Because of Smith's witless spike, the Steelers lost 6 sure points, while the Chiefs gained possession of the ball on the 20-yard line.

Adding misery to his embarrassment, Smith had to endure the hoots and hollers of the Chiefs as he ran past their bench on his way toward his own disbelieving teammates.

He blamed his blunder on "tough luck"—but Smith was just plain out of luck.

MICHIGAN WOLVERINES

Nov. 22, 1969

It's one thing to drop the ball, but to drop your coach?

That's what the Michigan Wolverines did to their mentor, Bo Schembechler.

In one of the school's biggest games ever, the Wolverines faced their undefeated arch rival—and the nation's No. 1 team—the Ohio State Buckeyes. Michigan sought revenge; in the fifteen years previous to 1969, they had been beaten by the Buckeyes eleven times.

In preparing for the game, Schembechler psyched his players up by making them each wear a tiny No. 50 on their jerseys during practice as a subtle reminder of Ohio State's 50–14 rout over them the year before.

By game time, the underdog Wolverines were snarling. They attacked the Buckeyes with a vengeance all day and trotted off the gridiron with a convincing 24–12 triumph. The Michigan players laughed it up, sang "Hail to the Victor," and waved a bunch of plastic red roses, a reference to their forthcoming trip to the Rose Bowl.

Then, before a roaring crowd of 103,588 at Michigan Stadium, the Wildcats hoisted Schembechler onto their shoulders for the euphoric victory ride to the locker room. But incredibly, the same players who performed so flawlessly on the field muffed the celebration. In one of the most embarrassing fumbles imaginable, they dropped Schembechler!

The unexpected fall aggravated an old football knee injury, but hardly hurt the coach's feelings. Recalled Schembechler, "It was the only thing those kids fumbled all day."

FLORIDA STATE SEMINOLES VS. WICHITA STATE SHOCKERS

Sept. 20, 1969

Florida State and Wichita State suffered the most virulent case of football's most dreaded disease—fumblitis.

They played as if the affliction was terminal. It obviously was infectious. The Shockers were the first to be plagued by the bobbles, but the Seminoles came down with the same ailment in the first quarter. Wichita State fumbled 17 times, losing the ball ten times, while Florida State coughed up the ball seven of the ten times it fumbled.

The teams' performance was so sick there was talk of calling the Center for Disease Control to curb a possible epidemic. As it was, the two mistake-riddled teams secured a place in the NCAA record books for a total of 27 fumbles in a single game.

The teams contracted fumblitis from the heavy downpour that drenched Doak Campbell Stadium in Tallahassee, Florida. More than five inches of rain turned the field into a quagmire of slithering, slippery, and skidding players. Complained Seminole receiver Kent Gaydos, who dropped a touchdown pass, "That ball hit me right on the button and it felt like a greased pig. I don't think I could have caught it with handles on it."

Surprisingly, only 10 points came as a direct result of the fumblitis. That's because both teams frittered away scoring opportunities by losing the ball. As it turned out, Wichita's condition was more critical than Florida State's, and the Shockers succumbed to the dropsies in a 24–0 defeat.

WOEFUL WINDUPS

Games, rivalries, seasons, and careers must all come to an end. Some finish gracefully. Others draw to a close without a shred of dignity, leaving behind a residue of shame that even the garbageman won't touch. For "The Most Disastrous Farewell Peformances," The Football Hall of SHAME inducts the following:

YALE BULLDOGS

Nov. 21, 1925

Yale has always been known for its students' high intelligence, but the school's 1925 football team showed a complete lack of brains in the final seconds of the year's biggest game.

Only a yard away from the winning touchdown, the Bulldog backfield bickered so long over what play to run that time expired! It was a witless windup to a scoreless tie against the arch rival Harvard Crimson.

Yale, the odds-on favorite to win big, totally dominated the game, racking up 252 total yards and 13 first downs to Harvard's 106 yards and 3 first downs. Yet the Bulldogs gave one of the greatest exhibitions of futility and wasted opportunity ever seen on a collegiate gridiron.

On 5 separate possessions, Yale had a first down inside the Crimson 10-yard line and failed to score. Twice the Bulldogs lost the ball on downs on the Harvard 2-yard line.

The Bulldogs played as though teamwork was a personal foul. They threw more cross words at each other than they did blocks against the Crimson. Yale employed two shuttling quarterbacks, who could not hold the team together long enough to drive over the Harvard goal. Throughout the first half, quarterback Dwight Fishwick squabbled openly with his backfield mates, who didn't want to run the plays he called.

But the stupidest spat came during the final seconds of the 0–0 deadlock after quarterback Phil Bunnell drove Yale to a first down at the Crimson 5-yard line. Bunnell sent Bruce Caldwell smashing into the line 3 straight times, bringing the Bulldogs to within a yard of the promised land and victory.

There was time for one more play. But rather than choose a field goal attempt or another plunge into the line, the backfield chose to fight— among themselves. While captain Johnny Joss quarrelled with Bunnell over what play to run, no one had enough smarts to call time-out. As the dispute raged on, the last seconds ticked off the clock.

Each team had scored zero—which, in the game's closing moments, was exactly the collective I.Q. of the Yale backfield.

CHICAGO BEARS VS. ROCK ISLAND INDEPENDENTS

October 17, 1920

When the fierce battle between the Chicago Bears and the Rock Island Independents ended, George Trafton faced an even more brutal challenge.

Trafton—the roughest, meanest, most ornery center ever to snap the ball for the Bears—was strongly disliked in every city in the NFL except Green Bay and Rock Island. In those cities, he was hated.

Playing in a particularly violent game in Rock Island, Trafton knocked four Independents out of action in the span of just 12 plays. Desperate to get even, Rock Island inserted a second stringer to act as a hatchet man with orders to dispose of Trafton by any means necessary. Minutes later, however, the Independent thug was carried off the field; Trafton's cleats had left bloody tracks from the man's forehead to his chin. The crowd, already angry over Trafton's tactics, erupted into further outrage when Trafton spun star fullback Fred Chicken out of bounds with such force that Chicken smashed into a fence and broke his leg.

When the final gun sounded, Trafton sprinted for the nearest exit. Passing the Bears bench, he grabbed a sweatshirt to hide his uniform number, but it did no good. The furious fans chased him out of the stadium and down the street while showering him with rocks and empty bottles.

Trafton leaped into a waiting cab, but when rocks came crashing through the windows, he jumped out and tried again to flee the crowd on foot. He finally managed to escape when a passing motorist, obviously not a Rock Island fan, gave him a lift.

Three weeks later, when the Bears returned to Rock Island for a rematch, the crowd was nearly as ugly and unruly. When the game ended, Bears owner George Halas was handed $7,000 in cash—his team's share of the gate receipts. He turned the money over to Trafton for safekeeping. Explained Halas, "I knew that if trouble came, I'd be running only for $7,000. Trafton would be running for his life."

TULANE GREEN WAVE VS. LOUISIANA STATE FIGHTING TIGERS

Nov. 26, 1938

In the most appalling ending ever to a collegiate football game, Tulane powered its way into the end zone by slugging, holding, and crackback blocking while LSU defended its goal by spearing, tripping, and clothesline tackling.

This mayhem was inflicted not by the players but by the fans!

When the final gun sounded in a 14–0 Green Wave victory in Tiger Stadium, it signaled the start of a violent free-for-all forever known as "The Big Blowout."

The spectators were primed to riot after watching a fierce, penalty-marred game that erupted into a fourth-quarter brawl between the two teams. Once peace was restored, both sides shook hands and played out the game without further fisticuffs.

But the fans hadn't had enough, and invaded the field as the clock ticked off the final few seconds. Tulane rooters charged after the goal posts to claim them as booty for their team's triumph. Meanwhile, LSU boosters swarmed into the end zone to protect their posts. Like clashing armies during medieval times, thousands waged hand-to-hand combat that left scores bruised, battered, and banged up. The outnumbered policemen could do little to quell the melee.

The band played several renditions of "The Star Spangled Banner" to try to stop the fracas, but nobody paid any attention as the battle flowed from one end of the field to the other. Skirmishes even flared up outside the stadium, where fans beat each other with frozen sugarcane sticks swiped from nearby fields.

Although the Tulane fans managed to tear down the goal posts, LSU supporters saved the posts and carted them away for safekeeping. But the conflict didn't stop. Everyone wanted a piece of the action—including waterboys, mascots, and even cheerleaders.

When the fighting was at its peak, a cute blond LSU cheerleader ran out of the seething throng to the sideline where Bernie Moore, coach of the Fighting Tigers, was standing. The girl's clothes were torn and she was bleeding from a cut on her face. "Coach," she said, "ain't we having fun?" Then she turned right around and ran back into the fray.

PAUL "SKEETER" GOWAN

Running Back ▪ Memphis State Tigers ▪ Dec. 18, 1971

After clawing his way to a touchdown in the final game of his collegiate career, Memphis State Tiger Paul "Skeeter" Gowan turned into a scaredy-cat.

During a game against the San Jose State Spartans in the Pasadena Bowl, which the Tigers won 28–9, the diminutive Gowan skirted left end and shook off two tacklers on his way to an 18-yard touchdown run in the fourth period.

Once in the end zone, Gowan slowed to a stop. But a burly and angry Spartan lineman who'd been in hot pursuit kept right on coming, so Gowan trotted out of the end zone. So did the lineman. When Gowan heard his pursuer yell, "I'm gonna get you!" that was the Tiger's signal to turn tail and run for safety.

"I could feel that heat coming right off him," Gowan recalled. "He wasn't going to stop and I wasn't going to let him knock me into the stands, so I just kept on running."

The little Memphis ball carrier raced eight rows up into the end-zone bleachers. When he turned around, he saw—much to his relief—that the riled Spartan had finally given up the chase.

Gowan sat down, placed the ball in his lap, and caught his breath. Then he tossed the pigskin back to the ref—but didn't budge from his seat. "I stayed for about 10 minutes," Gowan recalled. "I was in no hurry to get back down there and have that guy chase me again. After all, it was the last game I was ever going to play."

STANFORD CARDINALS VS. CALIFORNIA GOLDEN BEARS

Nov. 20, 1982

If the final play of the Stanford–California game had been a scene in a Disney film, it would have ended up on the cutting room floor for being too ridiculous—even by Goofy's standards.

The play defied description, defied imagination, defied logic.

Stanford had just vaulted into a 20–19 lead on a dramatic field goal with only 4 seconds remaining in the game. All the Cardinals had to do was kick off, tackle the return man, and celebrate the victory.

Kicker Mark Harmon deliberately squibbed the ball, and it bounced into the arms of Kevin Moen on the Golden Bears' 43-yard line. Moen zigzagged upfield and, just before being hit, lateraled to teammate Richard Rodgers at the Stanford 48-yard line. Then, as Rodgers was about to be tackled, he lateraled to Dwight Garner at the 44-yard line. Time had expired but the play was still alive.

Garner was stopped, but before he went down, he flipped the ball back to Rodgers. By now the field was filling up with fans, players from the Stanford bench, and members of the school's band who poured out onto the gridiron from the Cardinal end zone. They all thought the game was over. They were wrong.

When Rodgers was hemmed in by Cardinals, he tossed the ball back to trailing teammate Mariet Ford, who sprinted down to the 20-yard line. Then Ford threw the ball blindly over his shoulder in the faint hope that a fellow Golden Bear would catch it.

Sure enough, Moen, the player who started it all, was there to snatch the lateral on the dead run at the 25-yard line (next to the woodwinds). Meanwhile, by being on the field, the Stanford music makers unwittingly screened off potential tacklers. One Cardinal defender chased Moen, but eased off once he ran into the thick of the bewildered band members. But Moen continued to thread his way through the musicians, who began fleeing in all directions.

Moen dashed into the end zone, where he knocked down saxophonist Scott DeBarger and bowled over trombonist Gary Tyrrell for the most bizarre ending to a football game ever. California had used five laterals on a kickoff return with no time left to turn certain defeat into an unbelievable 25–20 victory.

On the Stanford sideline, coach Paul Wiggin waited for an official to call the play back. But the only call made was "touchdown." The play left the Cardinals wandering aimlessly on the field.

This was chaos. This was history. This was shame. "This was the biggest fiasco of all time," fumed Wiggin.

NORTH CAROLINA'S SUGAR BOWL DEFEAT

Jan. 1, 1949

North Carolina's loss in the Sugar Bowl tasted mighty bitter to the Tar Heels. What made it so hard to swallow was the woeful way they left Tulane Stadium.

In a game they were favored to win, the Tar Heels were tripped up by the Oklahoma Sooners 14–6.

Whooping and hollering with glee, the Sooners showered and dressed quickly. They were anxious to board their buses and return to their New Orleans hotel for a night of wild celebration.

Meanwhile, in the somber losers' locker room, the Tar Heels glumly took their time, trying to come to grips with the stinging upset. With their heads hung low, the players silently filed out of the stadium and into the parking lot. But it was deserted.

To their distress, they discovered that the buses assigned to them had already left. And to make matters worse, their buses had taken Oklahoma's cheering contingent by mistake.

After a futile search for the buses, coach Carl Snavely and some team members managed to wave down a passing truck. Like cattle, the players herded into the open back end of the truck and rode to within two blocks of the hotel. "Y'all have to get off here," said the driver. "I'm not allowed to drive to the entrance."

As darkness descended on New Orleans, the downtrodden Tar Heels slipped unnoticed into a side entrance of the hotel like busboys headed for work.

It was just as well. They were too embarrassed to be seen by even the doorman.

COLLEGE ALL-STAR GAME

July 23, 1976

It was an ignoble way to die.

Lightning raked the sky and solid sheets of driving rain cascaded onto Chicago's Soldier Field with such force that the two football teams scurried to the sidelines. Then thousands of soaked and soused fans surged onto the field, some harassing players and officials, others sliding and bellywhomping on the slick, wet surface like otters on an ice floe. Finally, gangs of rowdies risked electrocution by tearing down the metal goal posts.

Thus, with more than a quarter still to be played, the final College All-Star football game was called off.

For forty-three years, the annual contest had pitted the NFL champion against a team of the previous year's outstanding college seniors. The event drew huge crowds and earned millions of dollars for charity. But it also drew criticism. The collegians had failed to win any of the last 13 games and only rarely were they able to make the contest remotely interesting.

The 1976 game proved to be as boring as usual. The Pittsburgh Steelers held a commanding 24–0 lead in the third quarter. But then the fans were jolted out of their doldrums—and seats—by a violent thunderstorm that prompted officials to halt play. With 1:22 left in the period, the players were sent to the sidelines as a safety precaution.

Attempting to put excitement into a night when none was being provided by the All-Stars, 4,000 wild fans streamed onto the now-flooded field. They skidded, sloshed, and splashed around, playing a mock football game with the ball that the teams had left behind in their hasty exit.

But what started out as a frolic-filled lark turned into an ugly mob scene. Ignoring referee Cal Lepore's plea to clear the field, drunken hooligans began badmouthing and hassling the players.

"It was like Custer's Last Stand," declared Steeler quarterback Terry Bradshaw. "Those idiots came out, carrying their juice buckets, and surrounded us."

Both teams retreated to their locker rooms. Meanwhile, outside in the raging storm, fans tore down both metal goal posts and paraded with them, pointing then up toward the lightning-filled skies as if challenging the heavens to strike them.

After 20 minutes of mob rule, the officials had no choice but to make the unprecedented move of canceling the rest of the game. A feeling of anger and frustration spread through the All-Stars' locker room. "What do you think the feeling of the public would be if the players quit with 17 minutes left in the game? They'd raise hell," groused Wisconsin safety Steve Wagner. Added Oklahoma running back Joe Washington, "You expect fans to do stuff like that at the end of a game, but in the third quarter? Gollee!"

Eventually, more than 100 policemen formed a line and, like a human squeegee, wiped the unruly fans off the flooded field.

It wasn't long before the powers that be decided to lay the annual event to rest. The 1976 debacle was the College All-Star Game final performance, a swan song marred by too many sour notes.

DENNY CLARK

Halfback • Michigan Wolverines • Nov. 30, 1905

Denny Clark suffered the most lamentable ending ever to a collegiate football career.

He made a fuddle-brained blunder that cost his team not only its first loss in five years but also the conference championship. Clark's goof was further magnified by the fact that he had the misfortune of playing football in an era when victory was a matter of life and death.

To Clark, life just wouldn't seem worth living if the highly favored Michigan Wolverines lost to the University of Chicago Maroons in the Windy City. The game had turned into a surprisingly tense defensive struggle, and it looked as if it would end in a scoreless tie—until Clark lost his head.

With five minutes left in the game, the Maroons punted the ball into

the Michigan end zone. Clark, a substitute halfback, fielded the ball while his teammates shouted, "Down it!" and "Stand still!" All he had to do was down it, which, according to the rules back then, would have given Michigan possession of the ball on its own 25-yard line.

But Clark wanted to be a hero. He figured heroes don't play it safe. He quickly discovered that boneheads don't either. To the open-mouthed disbelief of the Wolverines, Clark darted out of the end zone—and smack into two Chicago tacklers, who drove him back across his goal line for a game-winning safety. It turned out to be the only score of the contest.

Immediately after the safety, Michigan's coach "Hurry Up" Yost took Clark out of the game. From that moment until he returned to the Ann Arbor campus the following day, the devastated Clark was sobbing and unconsolable. He said he couldn't bear to face the other members of his team, even though they all did their best to offer comfort and to assure him they weren't bitter. But apparently everyone else was.

One local newspaper headline read, "Clark 2, Michigan 0." Clark was ostracized on campus, flayed in the press, and broken in spirit. Within days, Clark quit school and sought seclusion in Michigan's barren north woods. There, in a lumber camp, he lived the life of a hermit, brooding over the mistake that had wrecked his career. It took years to coax him out of voluntary exile.

WHO ELSE BELONGS IN THE FOOTBALL HALL OF SHAME?

Do you have any nominations for The Football Hall of SHAME? Give us your picks for the most shameful, embarrassing, deplorable, blundering, and boneheaded moments in football history. Here's your opportunity to pay a lighthearted tribute to the game we all love.

On separate sheets of paper, describe your nominations in detail. Those nominations that are documented with the greatest amount of facts, such as anecdotes, firsthand accounts, newspaper or magazine clippings, box scores, or photos have the best chance of being inducted into The Football Hall of SHAME. Feel free to send as many nominations as you wish. If you don't find an existing category listed in *The Football Hall of SHAME* that fits your nomination, then make up your own category. (All submitted material becomes the property of The Football Hall of SHAME and is nonreturnable.) Mail your nominations to:

The Football Hall of SHAME
P.O. Box 6218
West Palm Beach, FL 33405

THE WINNING TEAM

BRUCE NASH has felt the pain of football shame ever since he tried to play quarterback in a sandlot game in West Palm Beach, Florida. He called for the "Quarterback Fake, Fullback Take." The center was supposed to hike the ball through Nash's legs to the player directly behind Nash. Unfortunately, the center snapped the ball straight up into Nash's crotch. From then on, the play was known as the "Quarterback Shriek." Today, Nash collects memorabilia from the World Football League, and he still talks about the greatest game he ever saw—when Wichita State and his alma mater Florida State fumbled a record twenty-seven times.

ALLAN ZULLO was an All-School-Yard receiver in Rockford, Illinois, where he was noted for his circus catches—he always looked like a clown. In high school, he tried out as a field goal kicker, but he was so bad he couldn't even split the uprights with an axe. As an expert on losers, Zullo is proud of his alma mater, Northern Illinois University, which did what no team had done against Northwestern in a record 34 straight games—lose. He has been rooting for the Tampa Bay Buccaneers ever since they dropped their first 26 games in a row.

Hall of Shame curator BERNIE WARD grew up idolizing the Kansas State Wildcats, who have only recorded one winning season in the last thirty years. During his high school playing days in Norton, Kansas, Ward was known as "B.D."—because he was the team's blocking dummy. Ward still believes Roy Riegels ran the right way and that Cumberland College should bring back football.